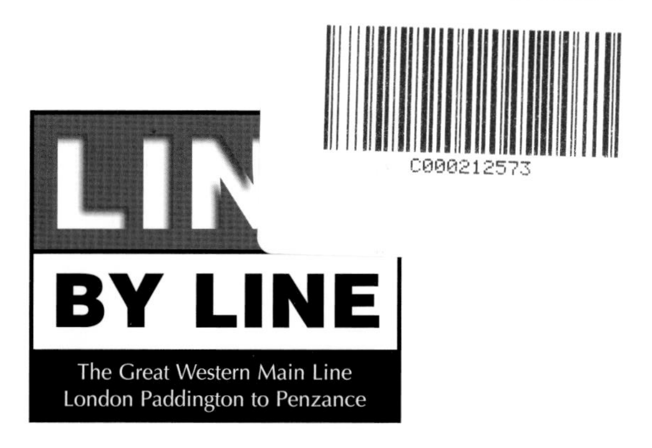

MARTIN BUCK

&

MARK RAWLINSON

Freightmaster
Publishing

CONTENTS

Schematic Maps & Research : Mark Rawlinson
e-mail : mark.rawlinson@virgin.net
fax : 01524-730591

Layout, Text & Captions : Martin Buck
e-mail : martin.buck1@virgin.net
fax : 01793-644079

ISBN : 0-9537540-1-4

Published by : Freightmaster Publishing
158 Overbrook
SWINDON SN3 6AY

Printed by : Tekprint Ltd., SWINDON

Front Cover Designed by : Tekprint Ltd.

Disclaimer: Every care has been taken to ensure accuracy and we believe all maps and tables are correct at the time of going to press; future developments will be accounted for when this edition is revised.

INTRODUCTION

THANK YOU for buying this copy of LINE BY LINE, the second book in our series of fully illustrated guides on famous railway routes. In fact, this volume should have featured the East Coast Main Line from London Kings Cross to Edinburgh but, due to public demand, we have brought forward the publication on the Great Western Main Line, so the East Coast book will follow at a later date.

THIS EDITION covers the route to the west of England from London Paddington to Penzance by way of the original Great Western Railway (GWR) main line via Bristol Temple Meads. We have also included the later 'Berks. & Hants.' link between Reading and Taunton.

Our long journey begins at Paddington station and the route is traced westwards in 5-mile sections until the end of the line at Penzance. All the regular features are included, such as Gradient Profiles & Topography, Track Plans and Mileage Tables.

CHANGES have been made to this edition,

Firstly, following numerous requests, the track plans now show where former lines and branches used to join the Great Western Main Line.

Secondly, we have increased the topographical scale to preserve an effective gradient profile. We have done this because, unlike the WCML which rises to a height of over 1,000 feet above sea level, the Great Western Main Line barely exceeds 450 feet at its highest point. Also, when the line climbs the Devonian and Cornish hills, there are frequent changes in gradient over relatively short distances and some of these are difficult to show clearly in a diagram. So, when this occurs, an average gradient has been shown instead to maintain clarity.

EVERY PAGE contains at least one recent photograph to illustrate a location of particular interest, so all parts of the route are featured. The photographs also provide representative coverage of the motive power and rolling stock associated with the Great Western Main Line in the late 1990s.

In addition, there is a special "Gallery" section, featuring high calibre colour photographs of classic photographic locations on both routes, plus full-colour reproductions of Ordnance Survey Landranger maps clearly showing the location of each view.

FINALLY we would like to extend our thanks to the photographers listed in the Glossary, who have kindly allowed us to use their excellent material, most of which has never been published before.

OVERVIEW

Background:

To many people, the main line from London Paddington to Bristol and onwards into Devon and Cornwall, can only mean one thing – the Great Western Railway or God's Wonderful Railway as some have christened it! It's a route which conjures up a magic all of its own: Broad Gauge, Brunel, diesel hydraulic locomotives, Castles and Kings, not to mention famous trains, such as the "Bristolian" and "Cornish Riviera Express".

The GWR is renowned for its great earthworks, such as Sonning Cutting and Box Tunnel, not to mention over 60 viaducts spanning more than 6 miles in length! It is also a route of contrasts, the first half is relatively level, but from Taunton it takes on a different complexion altogether with gradients posing a new challenge to locomotives and train crew alike.

Historical Perspective:

Of the four main British railway companies to emerge from the 1923 Grouping, the GWR was the only one to absorb others and retain its original identity. Of course, the GWR was always unique, starting off as a 7ft. 'Broad' gauge railway, the brainchild of one man – Isambard Kingdom Brunel, the Engineer of the Great Western, Bristol & Exeter, South Devon, Cornwall and West Cornwall Railway companies, who between them constructed the railway line from Paddington to Penzance.

The main line from London to Bristol was laid down in the 1830s, but by 1846 a new Gauge Act decreed that all new railways had to conform to a standard gauge of 4ft 8in. By 1859, the maximum mileage of the broad gauge had been reached and slowly the new standard gauge took over. Brunel died that same year aged 53, only months after the opening of probably his most famous engineering accomplishment, the bridge over the Tamar at Saltash.

The section of the Bristol & Exeter Railway over the Blackdown Hills was opened in 1844 and by May 1859 Plymouth had been linked to Truro, with a deviation to the original route between Saltash and St Germans constructed in 1908. The Hayle Railway opened to Redruth in 1837; it was rebuilt and extended, becoming part of the West Cornwall Railway, opening from Penzance to Truro (Newham quay terminus) in 1852 - the Cornwall Railway provided an extension through Higher Town Tunnel to the present station at Truro.

1935 was the Silver Jubilee of King George V and the centenary of the GWR, the Great Western Railway Bill having received the Royal Assent on August 31st, 1835. In October 1935, at a centenary banquet held in Grosvenor House, London, the Prince of Wales recalled how the GWR had provided a link between the Sovereign and the Government. This is the reason the GWR was known as "The Royal Road", notwithstanding the fact that it was on the GWR Queen Victoria first experienced rail travel and on it she made her last journey home.

Following nationalisation in 1947, the GWR became the Western Region of the newly-formed British Railways, contributing to the 1955 Modernisation Plan by introducing a four-number code in 1958 to describe trains in the working timetable.

This became the basis for a national system of train reporting codes, incorporating two numbers and two letters. Diesel locomotives displayed the codes in illuminated front panels with the same codes displayed by train describers in the latest signalling panels. These 'headcodes', as they became known, are still used today by the operating authorities, albeit sadly no longer displayed by locomotives.

From a signalling perspective, the Western Region began the task of upgrading its signalling system to multiple-aspect colour lights (MAS) starting with a new panel signalbox at Plymouth, opening for use in November 1960 and resulting in the closure of six mechanical boxes – a foretaste of things to come!

Attention was then switched to the main line out of Paddington with new power signal boxes (PSBs) being commissioned at Old Oak Common, Slough and Reading. Further west, a power signal box at Swindon controlled from Challow to Corsham and when the Swindon panel was linked to a new panel at Bristol in 1970, it completed a chain of colour light signals right through from Paddington to Bristol.

By March 1972, the Bristol signalling panel had been extended to Cogload Junction and the Plymouth panel linked Totnes and St. Germans in May 1974. By 1983, the building of Exeter PSB was well in hand, although it wasn't until November 1987 that resignalling was complete from Taunton through to Totnes, when Plymouth linked up with the panel at Exeter.

Signalling is an anachronism west of Plymouth as some 70 of the 80 odd miles to Penzance are still controlled by manual frame signal boxes and lower quadrant signals, although railway enthusiasts and Great Western aficionados are not complaining!

On the locomotive front, in 1837 Brunel had taken on a locomotive engineer by the name of Daniel Gooch, who by 1846 had designed and built at Swindon railway works a new express engine named 'Great Western', which was the prototype of the class during the broad-gauge era. Gooch died in 1889 and three years later the last broad-gauge train left Paddington for Penzance.

Of course, Swindon railway works was renowned for its locomotive design. In May 1904, 3440 City of Truro achieved a record-breaking speed of 102.3mph during the descent of Whiteball, whilst working the 'Ocean Mail' from Plymouth to London. Swindon also had the distinction of building the first diesel hydraulic main line locomotive in 1958 and British Railways last steam engine, 92220 Evening Star in 1960.

In the late 1970s, the introduction of the High Speed Train (HST) onto the Western Region of what was now British Rail revolutionised rail travel, speeding up services and eliminating most loco-hauled services at a stroke. Following the privatisation of British Rail in the mid-1990s, the new operator of the route decided to capitalise on past glories by adopting the name 'First Great Western'.

Passenger services today are still mostly operated by HST sets, although the possibility of a gas turbine 'Jet Train' replacement is being investigated. As for freight services, the class 66 locomotive has a virtual monopoly.

The Route itself:

PADDINGTON to BRISTOL TEMPLE MEADS:

London's **PADDINGTON** station was designed by Brunel in 1854. Lying in a valley aligned towards the Serpentine in Hyde Park, it is renowned for its splendid canopy roof. During recent years the station forecourt, known as the 'lawn', has been developed to provide improved passenger amenities, which has resulted in the buffer stops being moved westwards by five chains!

Leaving the station behind, the line passes through Ladbroke Grove, scene of a rail crash in October 1999, where 31 passengers died as a result of a Turbo express unit colliding with a Paddington-bound HST. Old Oak Common looms on the up side of the line, once a major locomotive maintenance depot, now used mainly for storing locomotives and home to the new 'Heathrow Express' electric units. Opposite, is the expansive North Pole 'Eurostar' depot.

At **Acton**, a freight yard stages aggregate trains from the Mendips, while a mile further west is **Ealing Broadway**, a station which also acts as the terminus for the Central and District lines of the London Underground. The main line then crosses Wharncliffe viaduct, across the Brent valley, notable for its impressive red brick arches. Shortly after **Hayes and Harlington**, the lines to Heathrow Airport diverge, the up line crossing the fast lines via a new flyover, which marks the current limit of electrification on the Great Western Main Line.

Slough was the first station in the country to be served by slip-coach, commencing in 1858 and just west of **Twyford**, the line passes through **Sonning Cutting**. Originally constructed for two broad gauge tracks, the cutting was widened to accommodate four standard gauge lines in 1893, following the abandonment of the broad gauge. Beyond lies **Reading**, a major interchange station with services to Birmingham, the south coast and also the point where the 'Berks. & Hants.' route to Taunton parts company with the Great Western main line.

Quadruple track continues through the Thames valley to **Didcot**, where the cross-country route to Oxford and Birmingham diverges under the shadow of the power station's massive cooling towers. **Steventon** is not only site of the first closed station out of London but also the location of the only two remaining level crossings between Paddington and Bristol.

The 'Golden Valley' route to Gloucester leaves the main line at **Swindon**, where the shell of the GWR railway workshops stands testimony to a former era. However, all is not doom and gloom as the site has been developed into one of the most successful retail shopping centres in the country and is the new home for Swindon railway museum.

After Wootton Bassett, junction for South Wales, the line descends 'Dauntsey Bank' and continues through **Chippenham** to reach **Box Tunnel**; the longest on the whole route at 1 mile 1452 yards long. The line from Bradford on Avon joins at Bathampton Junction before the Georgian splendour of **Bath** comes into view, with the Abbey holding centre stage.

At **BRISTOL TEMPLE MEADS** is Brunel's original 1840 station, one of the most important and impressive buildings of railway architecture, whose trainshed and tower were built to a Perpendicular Gothic style. In stark contrast to this magnificent sight, on the down side of the main line adjacent to the station, are the overgrown remains of Bristol Bath Road diesel depot.

BRISTOL to PLYMOUTH:

The line sweeps under Bath Road bridge and past the former Malago Vale carriage sidings where the Clifton suspension bridge, which spans the Avon gorge, can be seen to the west. Continuing deeper into Somerset, the junctions of Worle and Uphill are passed which mark the access points for the **Weston-super-Mare** loop.

At **Highbridge**, the Somerset and Dorset Line between Burnham-on-Sea and Evercreech Junction used to cross the main line by means of a flat crossing, although there are no signs of this remaining today. This section of track is straight and flat as the line crosses the fertile Somerset levels and over the Huntspill and King's Sedge Moor drain.

The 'Berks. & Hants.' joins by way of a 'dive under' junction at **Cogload** and the main line then continues into **Taunton**, the county town of Somerset, where passengers used to alight for local train services to Chard, Ilfracombe and Minehead. There were also intensive freight yards and a station avoiding line.

The main line climbs towards **Whiteball**, the first of three summits in Devon. The ascent includes inclines leading up to the Summit of 1 in 80 followed by a descent of 1 in 115 after passing through the tunnel. On the way to Exeter, the line passes through **Tiverton Parkway**, a relatively new station, located to provide better road connections, especially with the adjacent M5 motorway, which runs parallel to the main line for some 10 miles passing Cullompton on the way.

After following the River Culm, the line passes through the lower Exe valley between Pynes and Stoke Woods to reach Cowley Bridge Inn, a well-known landmark where the Barnstaple line trails in. Exeter Riverside yard is passed on the up side of the line adjacent to the River Exe, which is used primarily to stage freight trains on their journey to and from Cornwall.

Exeter St. David's station is where passengers interchange with services for Barnstaple, Exmouth, Torbay and stations on the line to Salisbury. In fact, the incline leading from the main line up to the ex-Southern Region station at Exeter Central is one of the steepest in Britain and, in steam days, trains required banking assistance in order to make the climb.

After leaving Exeter, the line follows the Exe estuary and along the coast through **Dawlish**, arguably one of the most spectacular stretches of main line anywhere in the country. The line continues to hug the coastline along the sea wall, past striking red sandstone cliffs, and on through a series of five tunnels to reach **Teignmouth**.

Shortly after **Newton Abbot**, two lines diverge for Torbay and the main line begins a climb to over 200ft at gradients as steep as 1 in 41 to **Dainton Tunnel**, before falling away equally as steeply to **Totnes**. The climb out of Totnes is also onerous, rising steeply up Rattery bank, until the summit is reached at **Wrangaton**. From there the line descends to Plymouth, including a 2-mile descent of Hemerdon at 1 in 42.

The ex-Plymouth & Dartmoor Railway joined the main line at Tavistock Junction, now the freight yard for the Plymouth area, principally handling china clay wagons for Marsh Mills. At Laira Junction, the lines leading to the maintenance depot and carriage sidings come into view, home to over 40 First Great Western and Virgin HST train sets.

The line then climbs up through Mutley Tunnel and into **PLYMOUTH** whose station, although on the GWR main line, was shared by the London & South Western Railway until their own station at Plymouth Friary was ready in 1891.

PLYMOUTH to PENZANCE:

The main line meanders through the built up areas of **Devonport** and **Keyham**. At St. Budeaux Junction, the branch line to Gunnislake diverges and immediately passes under the main line, only to reappear later passing underneath the **Royal Albert Bridge** on the Devon side of the River Tamar.

Brunel's famous bridge really is a magnificent sight, from where there are splendid views across to Devonport and its huge dockside cranes along with any warships anchored in Hamoaze water.

Into Cornwall and past **Saltash**, the line passes Trematon Castle and across the truly impressive Forder Viaduct spanning the River Lynher, one of over 30 viaducts the line crosses before reaching Penzance. As the line leaves St. Germans, signalling comes under the control of Liskeard and the first appearance of semaphores and signalboxes!

Looking to the North from Liskeard Viaduct, a single-track line curves round the valley below, on a 1 in 40 gradient, and comes back to pass under the viaduct. This is the Looe branch, which leaves **Liskeard** from a small terminus platform, once part of the Liskeard & Caradon Railway.

On leaving Liskeard, the main line climbs towards Doublebois (meaning 'two woods') and through a densely wooded area, crossing a series of 8 viaducts, the highest of which is St. Pinnock viaduct at 151ft. From **Lostwithiel**, china clay from the many clay dries in the area is 'tripped' down the Fowey branch to ECC's export terminal at Carne Point.

Some of the best examples of GWR manual frame signal boxes and lower quadrant semaphore signals can be seen at Lostwithiel and Par. **Par** is also the base for EWS freight operations in Cornwall and a servicing depot, complete with locomotive turntable, is located at St. Blazey. China clay is also exported from Par harbour, built by Joseph Treffry, who also built a line through the Luxulyan Valley to Newquay, to become the Cornwall Minerals Railway.

From Par, the line then climbs to Burngullow through **St. Austell**, a well-kept station displaying flowers, shrubs and even palm trees, a sign of the mild climate, which gives the Cornish 'Riviera' its name. Half the section of line from Burngullow to Truro has been singled and can prove to be a 'bottleneck', especially if trains are running late. The view is dominated by the cathedral as the line reaches **Truro**, the county town of Cornwall having been accorded city status in 1877.

The Falmouth branch leaves at Penwithers Junction, from where the main line climbs, inclusive of a 3½-mile section of 1 in 80, to **Redruth**, the highest station in Cornwall. The landscape is now a contrast to that which has gone before, it is open and littered with the remnants of the Cornish mining industry. Passing Carn Brea, a monument stands on top of a hill to commemorate Francis Bassett, a famous miners' welfare campaigner.

The North Cornish coast comes into view as the line approaches **Hayle**, crossing a low but long viaduct, with the town and harbour below. After **St. Erth**, junction for St. Ives, the main line switches to the South coast, past Marazion, where the 250ft St. Michael's Mount sits proudly in Mounts Bay. The carriage sidings at Long Rock are passed before the buffer stops are reached at **PENZANCE** – the end of the Great Western Main Line.

The 'BERKS. & HANTS.':

The main line between Reading and Taunton, known as the 'Berks. & Hants.', does not actually pass through the county of Hampshire at any point, although the line follows the Berks./Hants. border for several miles.

The route evolved by connecting several existing lines; the first section was built in 1847 from Reading to Hungerford and extended to Devizes in 1862. The London to Weymouth (via Chippenham) line already passed through Westbury and Castle Cary, whilst a branch line from Yeovil to Durston (near Cogload) was opened in 1853. So, only 29 miles of new track had to be laid – Patney to Westbury and Castle Cary to Curry Rivel.

Opened to passenger services in 1906, the route does not pass through any sizeable town after Newbury and the only gradient worthy of mention is the climb over the Mendip hills between Frome and Castle Cary. Of course, between Southcote Junction and Pewsey, the main line skirts the Kennet & Avon Canal to provide passengers with a pleasing vista through the carriage window as the line passes through Berkshire and Wiltshire.

Of particular note are the Westbury and Frome by-pass lines, constructed in 1933, to remove delays caused by the 30mph passage through both stations. By September 1978, colour lights had replaced semaphore signalling as far as Westbury where the construction of a new signalling centre had started in 1981. However, it was not until March 1987, when Taunton East was taken out of use, that Westbury finally linked up with Exeter power signal box.

Today, the route is also associated with carrying huge tonnages of stone from the Mendip Hill quarries at Merehead and Whatley. Although these freight services come under the control of EWS, the wagons and locomotives (Class 59s) and logistical control are provided by Mendip Rail, a company formed for the purpose of supplying the rail connected customers of Merehead and Whatley in the most efficient way.

Now turn the page and retrace the journey in more detail, LINE BY LINE.

LEGEND

An Overview

In compiling this book, the route has been split into five-mile sections, with one section per page. Each section comprises:

- A gradient profile
- A track plan
- A photograph

The Gradient Profiles

These show a 'cutaway' side-on view of the section, exaggerated enough to clearly show the changing gradients of the route. There is a vertical scale, marked in 200 foot increments and the highest point on the Great Western Main Line is only 455 feet above sea level at Wrangaton.

The Track Plans

These show a 'birds eye' view of the route, with running lines, junctions, etc. clearly marked. It should be noted that these plans are schematic and, while the maps themselves are to scale, certain features have had to be slightly enlarged to maintain clarity.

Key to Symbols

To make the diagrams in the following pages easy to use, symbols and abbreviations have been kept to the absolute minimum:

(grey bar)	=	station platform (in use)	*U.G.L.*	=	Up Goods Loop
(open bar)	=	station platform (disused)	*D.G.L.*	=	Down Goods Loop
SB	=	signal box	*U.P.L.*	=	Up Passenger Loop
PSB	=	power signal box	*D.P.L.*	=	Down Passenger Loop
⊠	=	disused signal box	(dotted line)	=	boundary between signal box areas

Paddington to Penzance

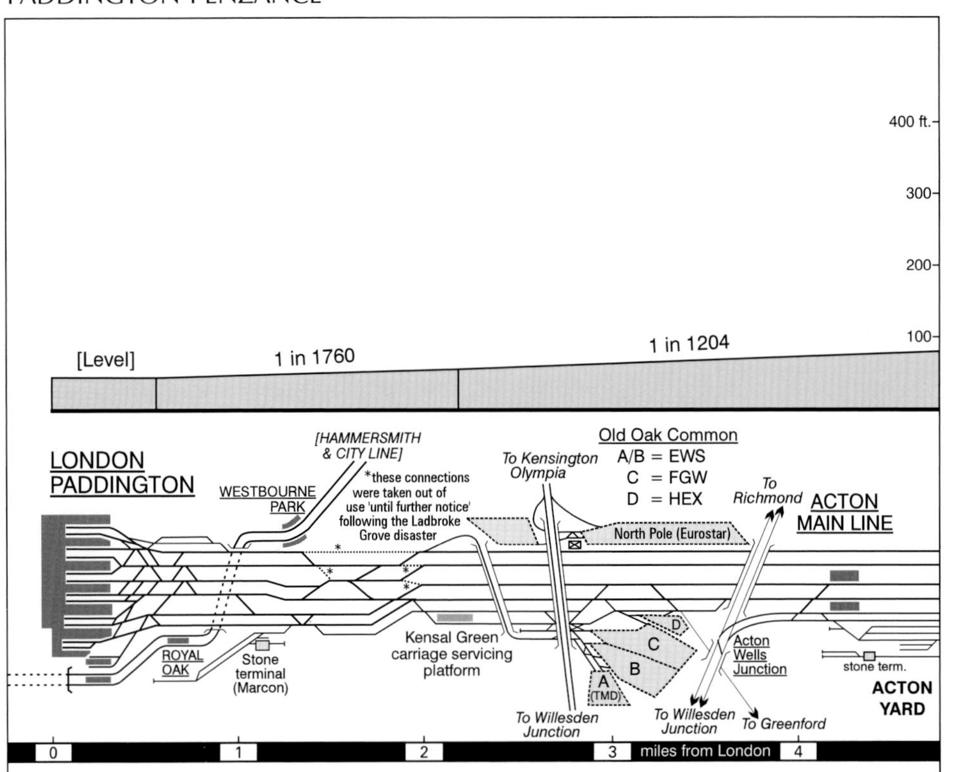

LONDON PADDINGTON : The starting point of our journey is Paddington station and a view which clearly shows the splendid canopy roof, plus the famous three-sided clock, albeit with only two faces showing. Two *Great Western Trains* High Speed Train (HST) sets along with a *Thames Trains* Turbo Express unit are also featured; these HSTs and Second Generation DMUs provide the backbone of services at this busy London terminus at the time of writing. (BM 05/98)

ACTON : A new class 67 locomotive, No. 67005 (above), heads 1V33, the 1558 London to Plymouth mail train 'down the bank' at a mandatory 10mph and onto the Great Western Main Line at Acton East Junction. The 'bank' gives access to the former Eastern, Midland and Southern Regions. (MB 05/00)

The yard to the north of Acton Main Line station is an important staging point for stone trains from the Mendip quarries bound for terminals in and around London and the South East. In this view, Hanson-liveried 59103 *Village of Mells* (below) and ARC-liveried 59101 *Village of Chantry* leave the yard hauling 7C75, the 1250 Acton to Whatley. (BM 01/99)

EALING BROADWAY : The station at Ealing Broadway is shared by London Underground, where tube stock can be seen to the right of 37194 *British International Freight Association* as it proceeds along the up relief line with steel empties from Wolverhampton to Hoo Junction. (BM 01/98)

HANWELL : This station retains splendid examples of Victorian architecture, especially the well preserved gas lamp holders on the platforms, which 60040 passes with 6M54, the 1230 Thorney Mill to Bardon Hill stone hoppers. (BB 04/00)

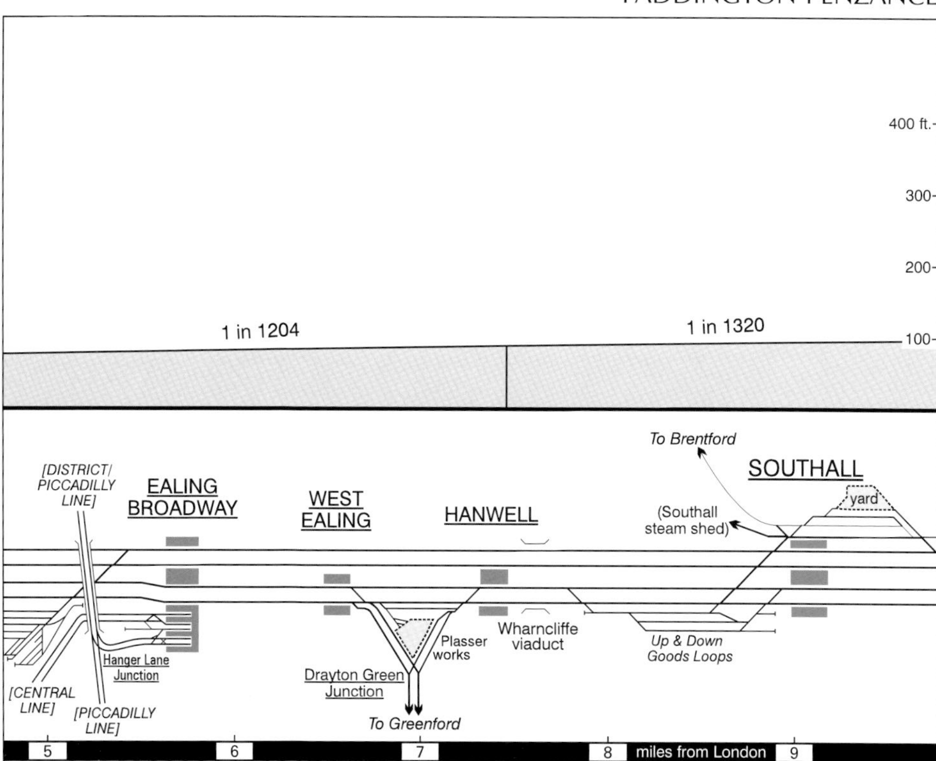

SOUTHALL : 'Heathrow Express' unit 332008 hurries through Southall with a train from Heathrow to Paddington and past two well-known landmarks: the gasometer and folly. On a more sombre note, Southall was the site of a major rail crash in September 1997 when an HST collided with a late running stone train at Southall East Junction and a total of seven passengers lost their lives with a further 139 injured. (BM 01/98)

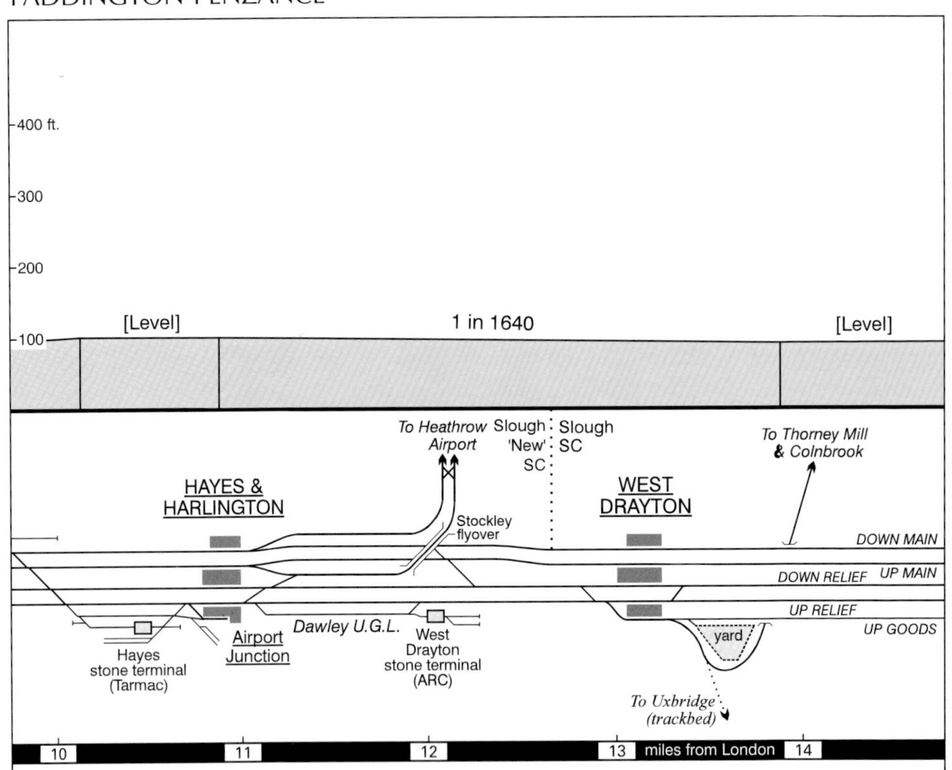

IVER : A regular freight flow is the transportation of Land Rover cars from Bordesley in the West Midlands to Dollands Moor for export. This train (6O95, the 0959 Washwood Heath to Dollands Moor) is seen passing through Iver station in Buckinghamshire on a stretch of the Great Western Main Line which is unique as there are five running lines between here and West Drayton. (MB 05/00)

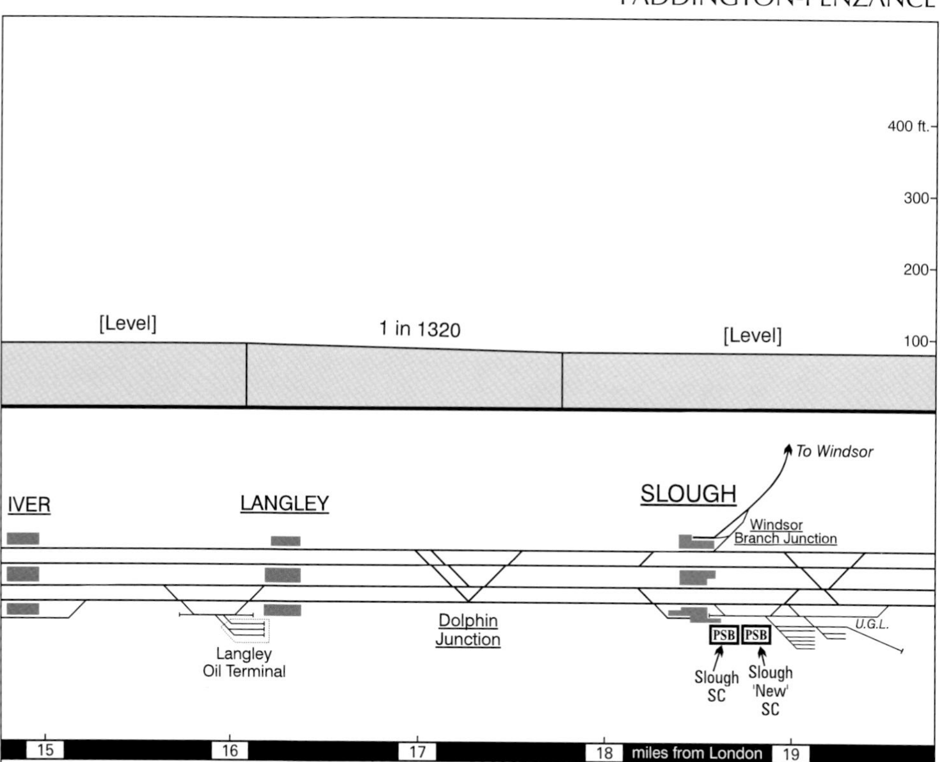

SLOUGH : As it makes the Slough station stop, 47851 is seen at the head of 1S87, the 1418 Paddington to Glasgow Central, passing the bay platform to the right of the picture which serves the single track branch line to Windsor & Eton Central. (BB 04/00)

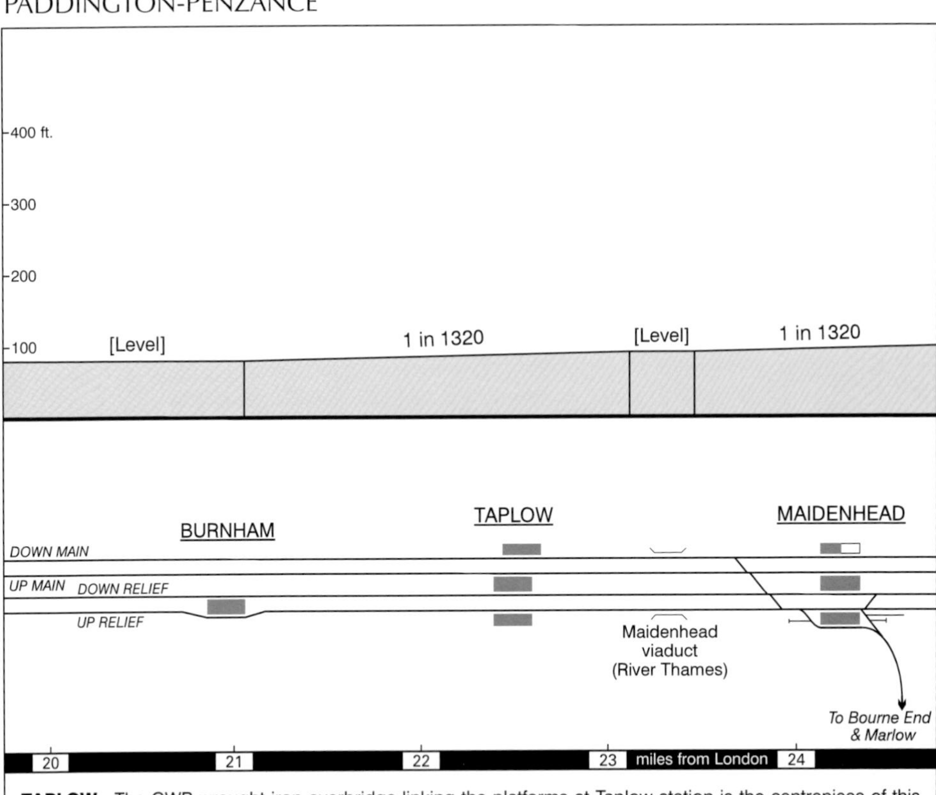

TAPLOW : The GWR wrought iron overbridge linking the platforms at Taplow station is the centrepiece of this picture in which we see 166214 passing under as it proceeds along the down slow line with the 1337 Paddington to Oxford service. (BM 03/00)

400 ft.
300
200
1 in 1320
100

Slough SC : Reading SC

Ruscombe U.G.L.

25 26 27 28 miles from London 29

RUSCOMBE : Substituting for the booked VXC class 47/8 locomotive, 47747 *Res Publica* on 1O30, the 0620 Preston to Brighton passes an HST on 1B24, the 1100 Paddington to Swansea at Ruscombe. Note the diamond shaped milepost marker at the side of the down main line. (BM 03/00)

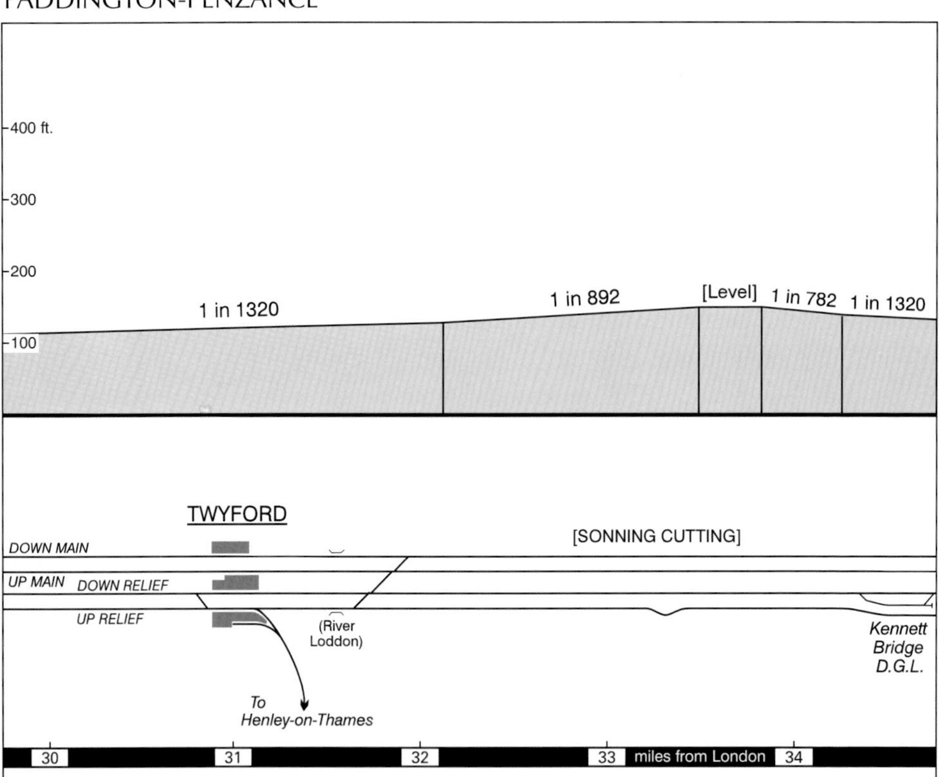

TWYFORD : Class 59 No. 59001 *Yeoman Endeavour* passes through Twyford with 7A09, the 0705 Merehead to Acton stone train, consisting of box wagons. (BM 04/98)

SONNING CUTTING : These two photographs were taken from bridges spanning Sonning Cutting, which give a good indication of how deep the cutting is. The first view from Bath Road bridge shows 59004 *Paul A Hammond* (above) passing milepost 33½ with 7C75, the 1248 Acton to Whatley stone empties, with some wagon numbers clearly visible. (BM 03/00)

Bath Road bridge is in the background as an HST (below) makes its way towards the Capital, forming 1A31, the 1130 Swansea to Paddington. Note how the cutting sides were cut back and retaining walls built to obtain more space; the original broad gauge tracks were under the middle arch. (BB 03/00)

READING : The bay platforms at the east end of Reading General station are provided with third rail electrification for services using the former Southern Region route to London Waterloo. In the view (above), 4-Cep unit (1533) along with a 4-Vep (3414) are on Waterloo services, whilst 166206 (above) waits on the up main platform line with a Thames Trains service from Oxford to Paddington. (BB 03/00)

This panoramic view shows the pre-1999 station layout at Reading General, where celebrity 'Deltic' D9000 *Royal Scots Grey* (below) leaves with 1M20, the 0906 Paddington to Manchester Piccadilly; 47851 is coupled in behind to take over the service at Birmingham New Street. (BM 08/97)

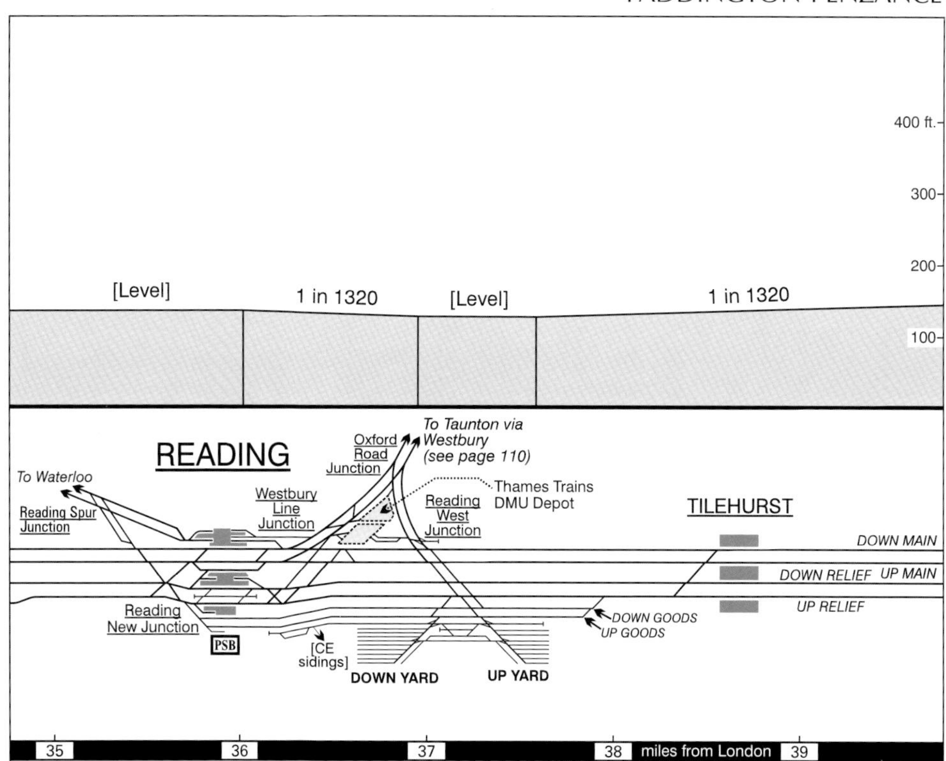

TILEHURST : The station buildings at Tilehurst still retain much of the former Great Western Railway architecture, illustrated in this view of 1O71, the 0736 Blackpool North to Portsmouth Harbour service, top 'n' tailed by 47843 and 47817. In the background is a wrought iron footbridge, built at Dudley in 1895, which leads to the River Thames. (MB 05/00)

400 ft.
300
200
100

1 in 1320

[Level]

(site of Goring water troughs)

PANGBOURNE

GORING & STREATLEY

DOWN MAIN

UP MAIN *DOWN RELIEF*

UP RELIEF

Gatehampton viaduct (River Thames)

40 41 42 43 miles from London 44

GORING & STREATLEY : A Network Turbo unit, No. 165137, pauses at Goring & Streatley station, whilst 57001 *Freightliner Pioneer* passes on the down relief line in charge of 4S59, the 1513 Millbrook to Coatbridge freightliner. Of note is the station footbridge, where the only remaining covered sections are over the steps leading down to the platforms. (MB 06/00)

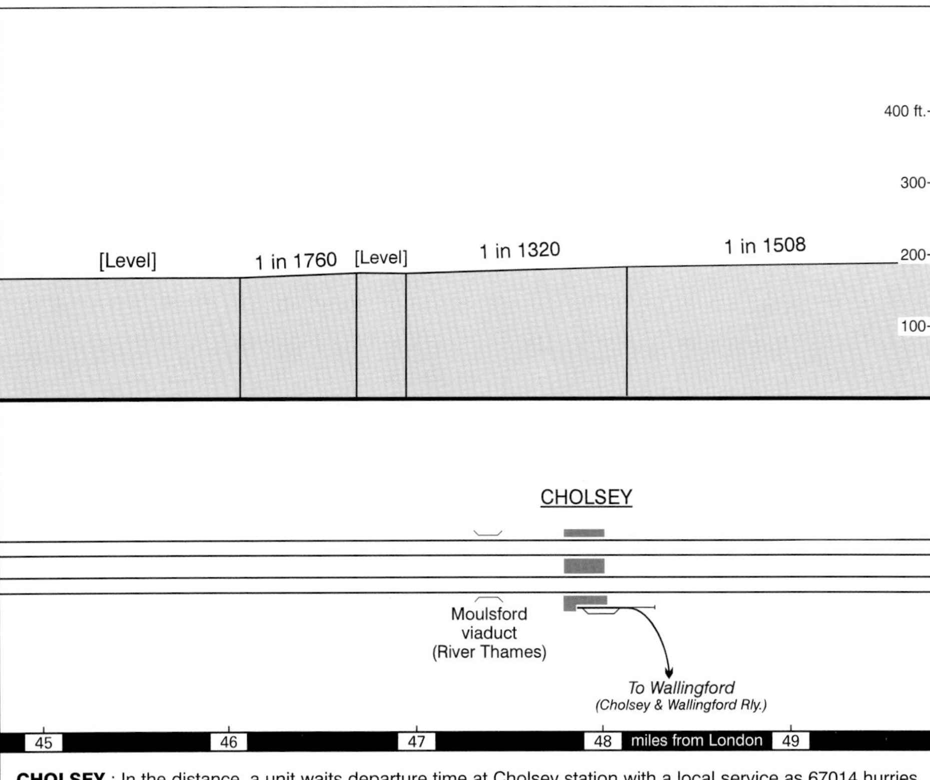

CHOLSEY : In the distance, a unit waits departure time at Cholsey station with a local service as 67014 hurries along the down main line in charge of 1V33, the 1558 London to Plymouth mail. (MB 05/00)

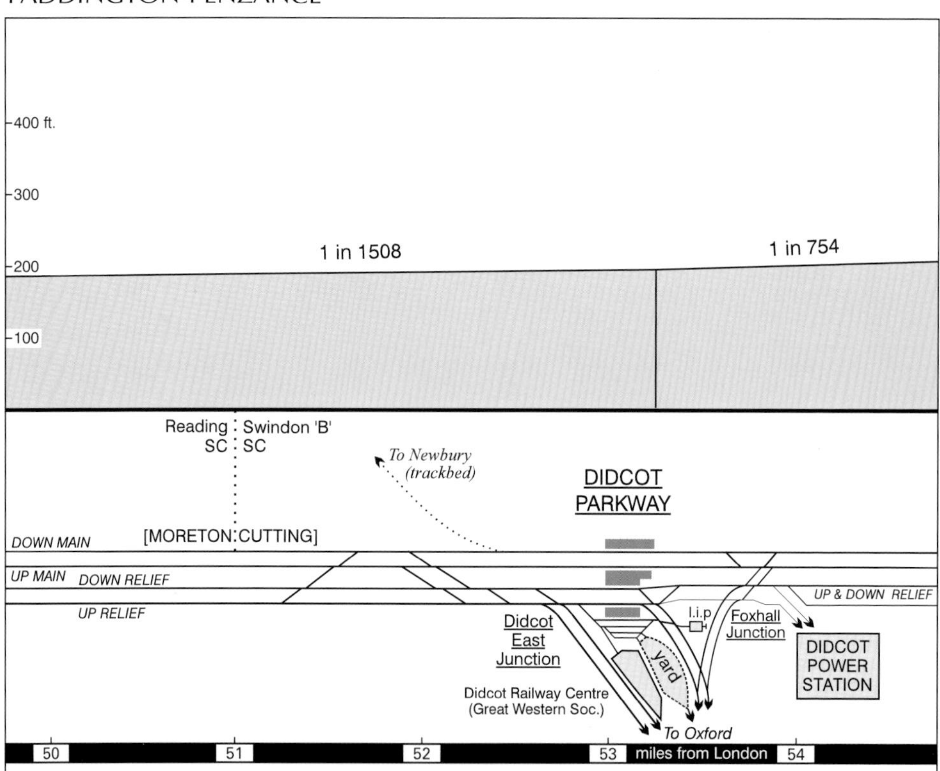

DIDCOT EAST : This location marks the start of a high-speed crossover, which enables inter-regional train services to leave the Great Western Main Line at Didcot East Junction and travel to Didcot North Junction and avoid the station altogether. In this view, a new crossover is being constructed in readiness for the introduction of *Virgin's* Voyager train services; 37372 towing a 'dead' class 58 locomotive, passes the site with 7O26, the 1027 Didcot yard to Eastleigh departmental. (PH 02/01)

DIDCOT : The power station cooling towers loom in the background behind Didcot yard in which three locomotives (above) are stabled: from left to right, 08904, 37047 and 37057 *Viking*. (MB 02/00)

In this panoramic view of Didcot Parkway, a Plasser unit proceeds along the down main, whilst 57003 *Freightliner Evolution* (below) negotiates Didcot West Junction in charge of 4E74, the 1231 Southampton to Leeds freightliner, having been unusually routed through the station. (MB 02/00)

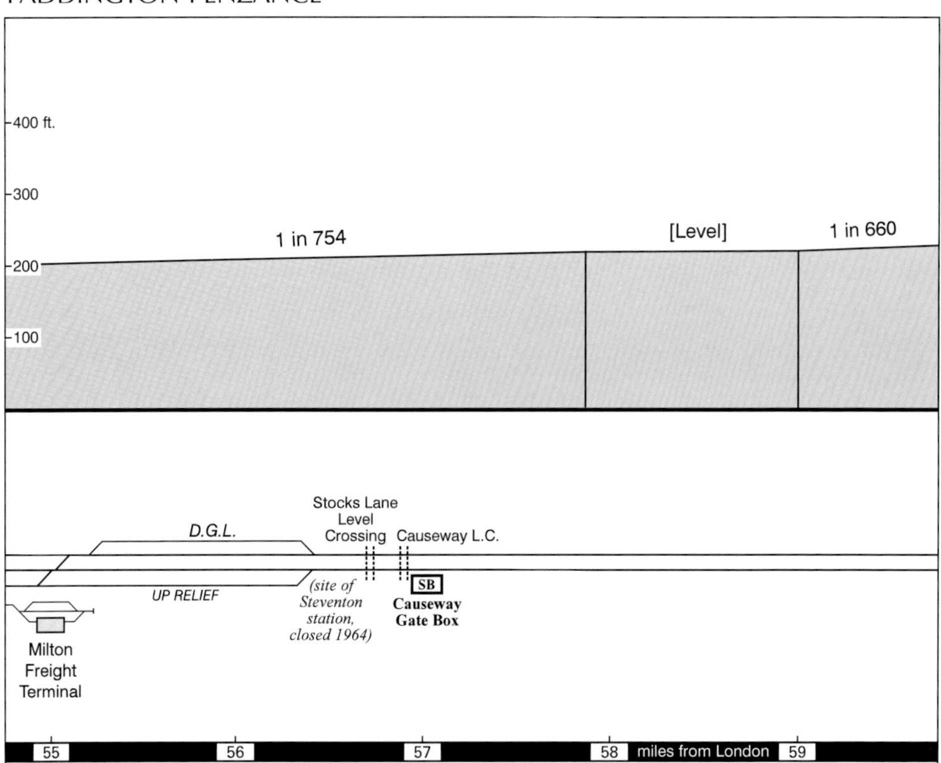

MILTON : Block trains of petroleum run from the Robeston refinery in South Wales to a terminal at Theale and the return empty bogie tanks 6B33, 1341 Theale to Robeston, are seen proceeding along the down goods loop at Milton on the outskirts of Didcot behind 60021 *Pen-y-Ghent*. (MB 05/00)

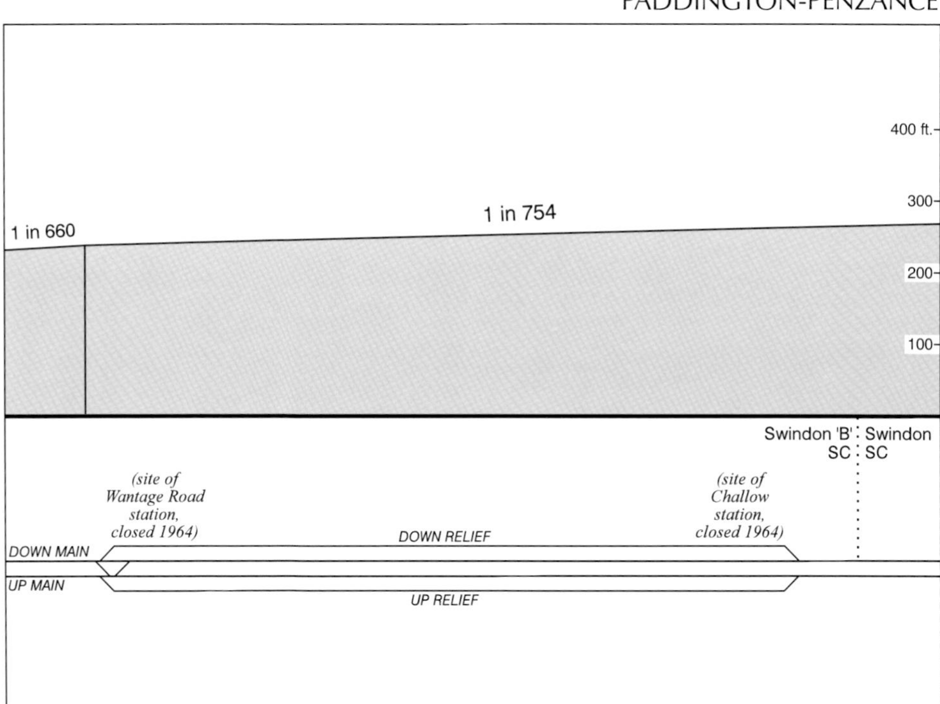

CHALLOW : The relief lines between Wantage Road and Challow are a recent addition to the main line, having been commissioned in 1993, ostensibly to cater for imported coal traffic from Avonmouth. Conversely, as a result, the nearby loops at Uffington were taken out. Having been switched to the up relief line, two mail vehicles en-route to Old Oak Common are seen passing the site of Challow station behind by 47752 on 5A24, the 0745 service from Barton Hill, Bristol. (MB 02/00)

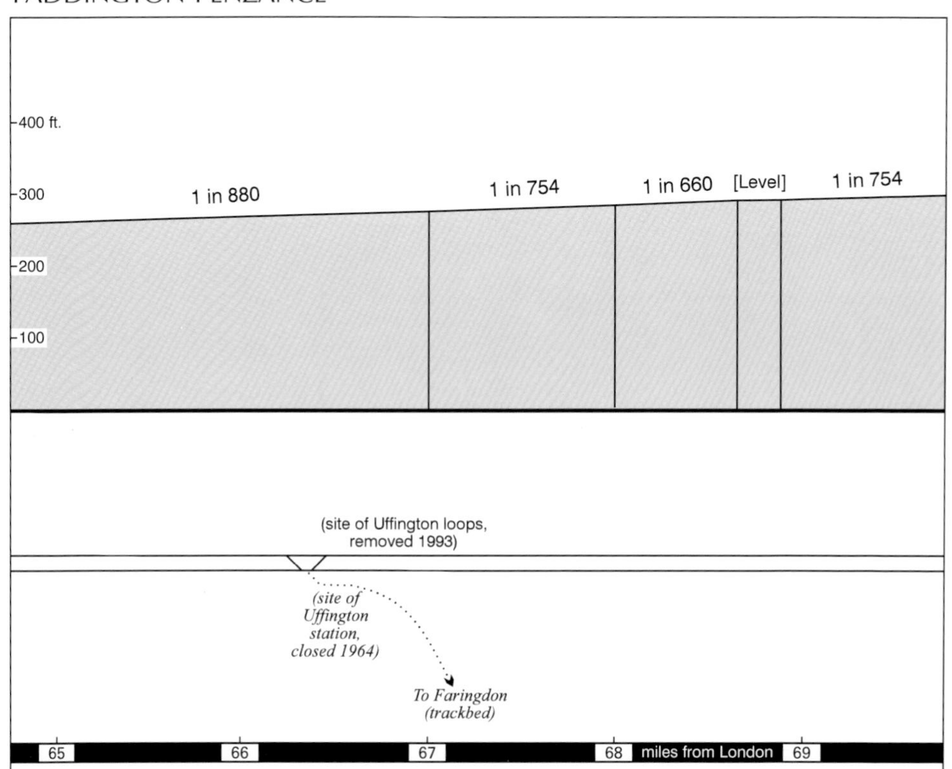

KNIGHTON : When the Western Region changed over from semaphore to colour light signalling, most level crossings between Swindon and London were replaced by overbridges. However, when Knighton crossing closed, the road was re-routed under the embankment which carries the main line where 47759 can be seen passing over with 1V33, the 1558 London to Plymouth mail. The old road was in the foreground, where two iron girders mark the spot and another view of this location is shown on page 6. (MB 04/00)

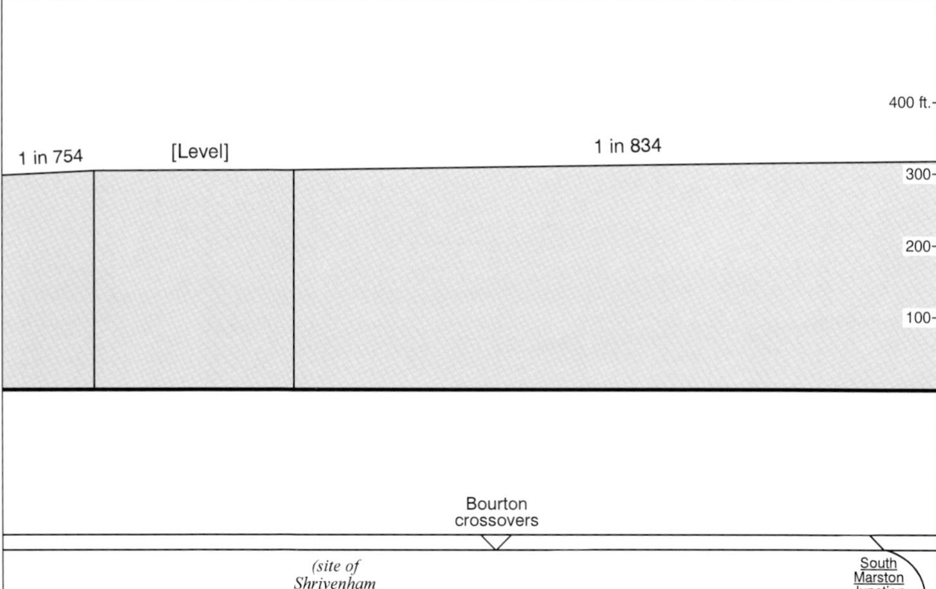

SHRIVENHAM : Running at restricted speed over newly laid track at Shrivenham, 60059 *Swinden Dalesman* passes the site of the old station at the helm of an MGR service of imported coal from Avonmouth Bulk Import Terminal to Didcot power station. (SM 02/98)

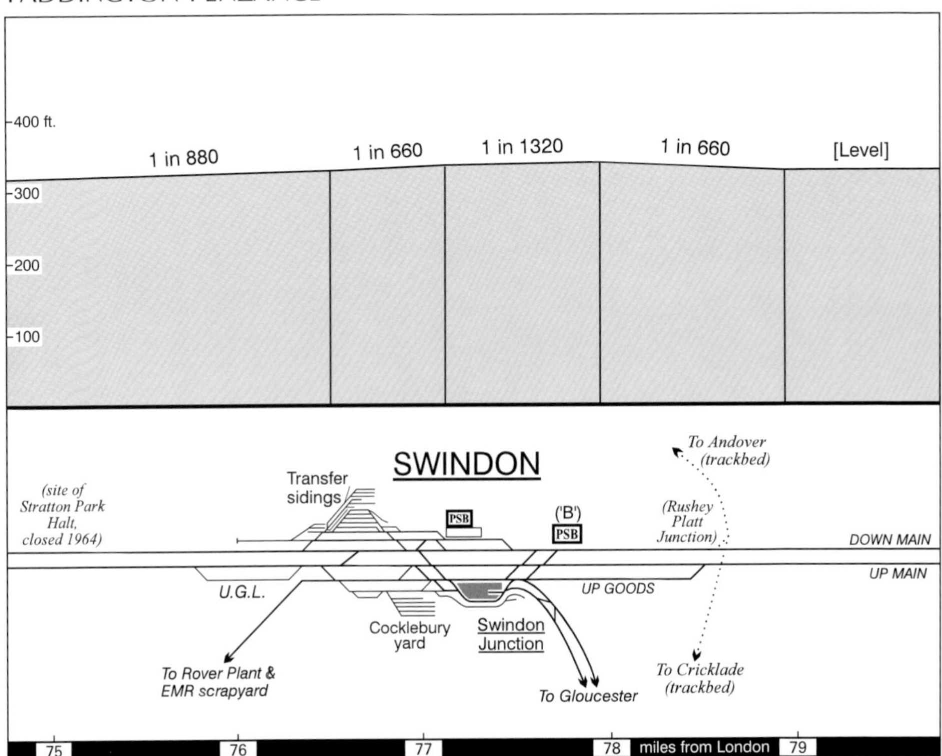

SWINDON : Photographed on an overcast day, typical of the Summer 2000 weather, 37219 heads onto the up main line at Highworth Junction, Swindon, with a lengthy 6A30, the 1324 Ashchurch to Didcot Yard MoD stores train. Note the MGR wagons stabled in the Transfer Sidings, due to a lack of capacity at Didcot. (MB 06/00)

SWINDON : Swindon station is an island platform situated adjacent to the main running lines. In the down loop, 37714 (above) waits departure with 4C13, the 1105 Calvert to Bath/Bristol Avon 'Binliner', which will follow behind 43009, seen arriving on 1B30, the 1300 Paddington to Swansea. (MB 02/00)

Unfortunately, apart from the administration building, only the facade is left of the former Great Western Railway workshops, visible (below) behind the bogie tanks in the consist of 6P82, the 2342 (sun) Robeston to Langley, hauled by 60090 *Quinag*. (MB 02/00)

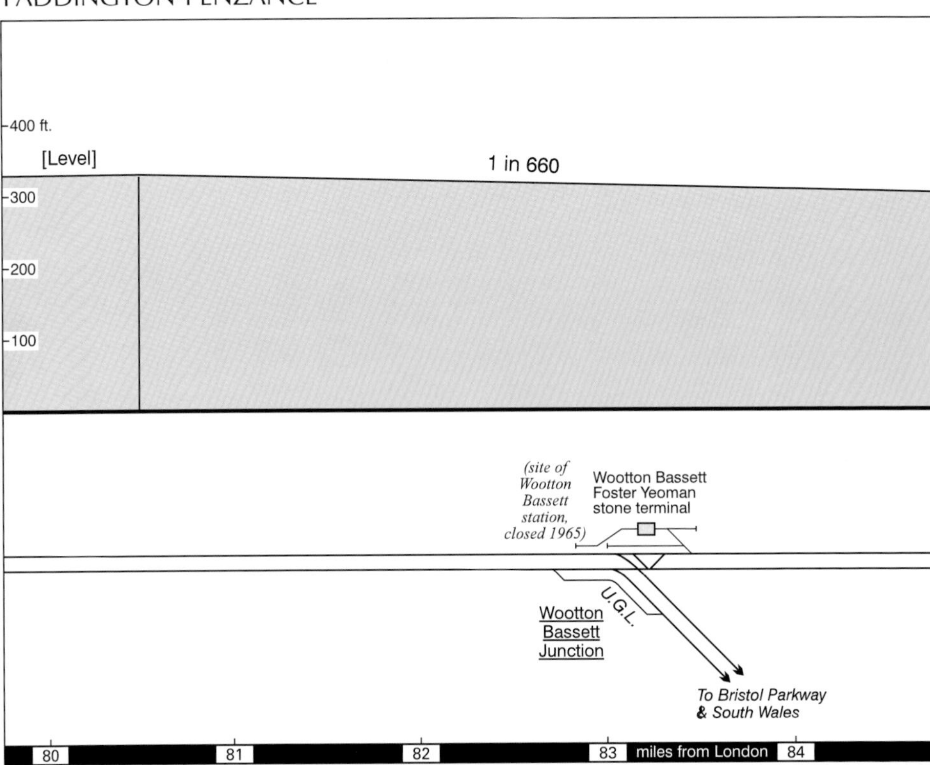

WOOTTON BASSETT : The main line to South Wales leaves the Paddington - Bristol route at Wootton Bassett Junction, partially visible to the left of the Turbo Express. The stone terminal at Wootton Bassett is depicted here where 66188, deputising for the booked class 59, makes its way through the discharge shed with 7B12, the 1345 service from Merehead. (MB 04/00)

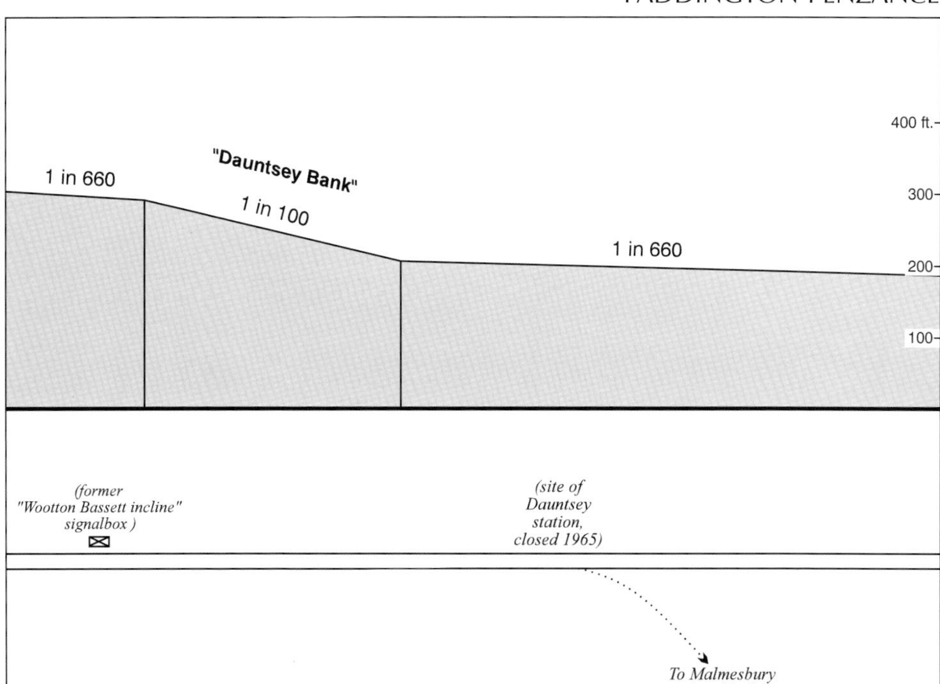

DAUNTSEY BANK : After passing milepost 85¾, close to the site of Wootton Bassett incline signalbox, a HST nears the end of the 1½ mile ascent up Dauntsey bank with 1C52, the 1545 Bristol Temple Meads to London Paddington. (MB 04/00)

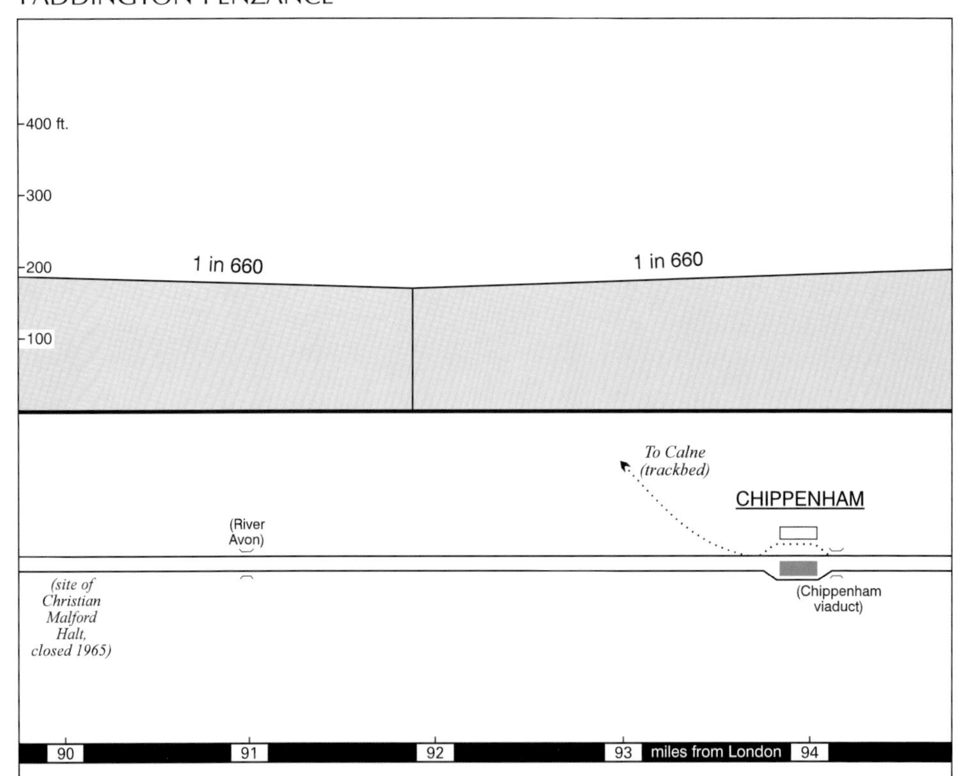

CHIPPENHAM : The market town of Chippenham, once junction for Calne, now handles only main line services using an island platform. On the down platform line, 43012 awaits to depart with 1C59, the 1645 Paddington to Bristol, whilst 165133 forms a service from Bristol to Bicester. Note the famous Westinghouse Brake and Signal factory partially visible in the distance. (MB 04/00)

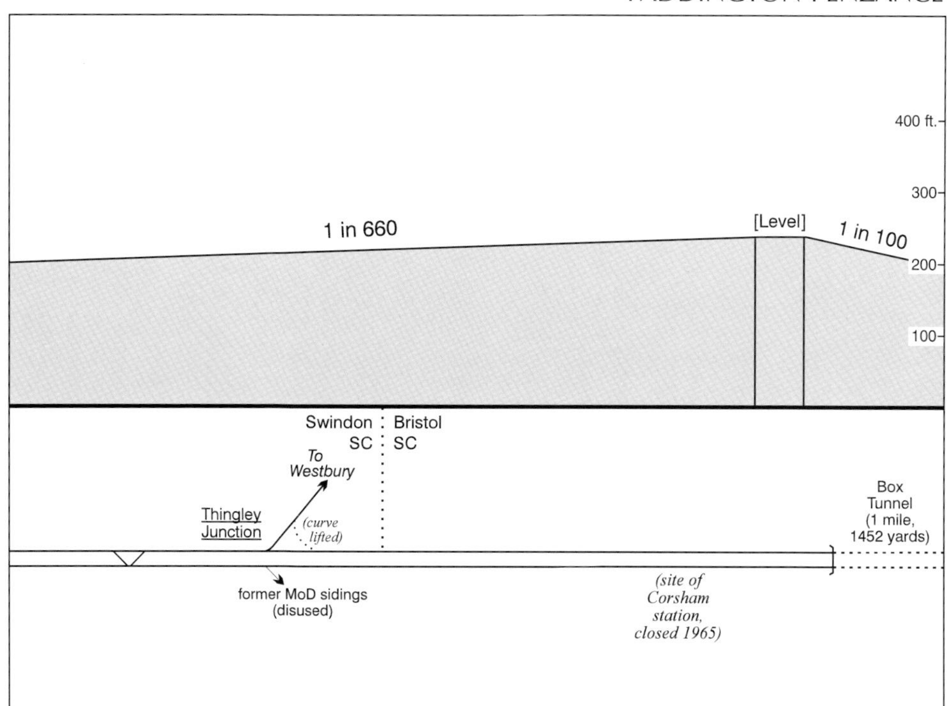

THINGLEY JUNCTION : The branch to Melksham leaves the Great Western Main Line at Thingley Junction, visible in the background, as 66158 heads the 'Binliner' past the former MoD sidings, where rusted steam locomotive boilers can be seen on the ground. (MB 04/00)

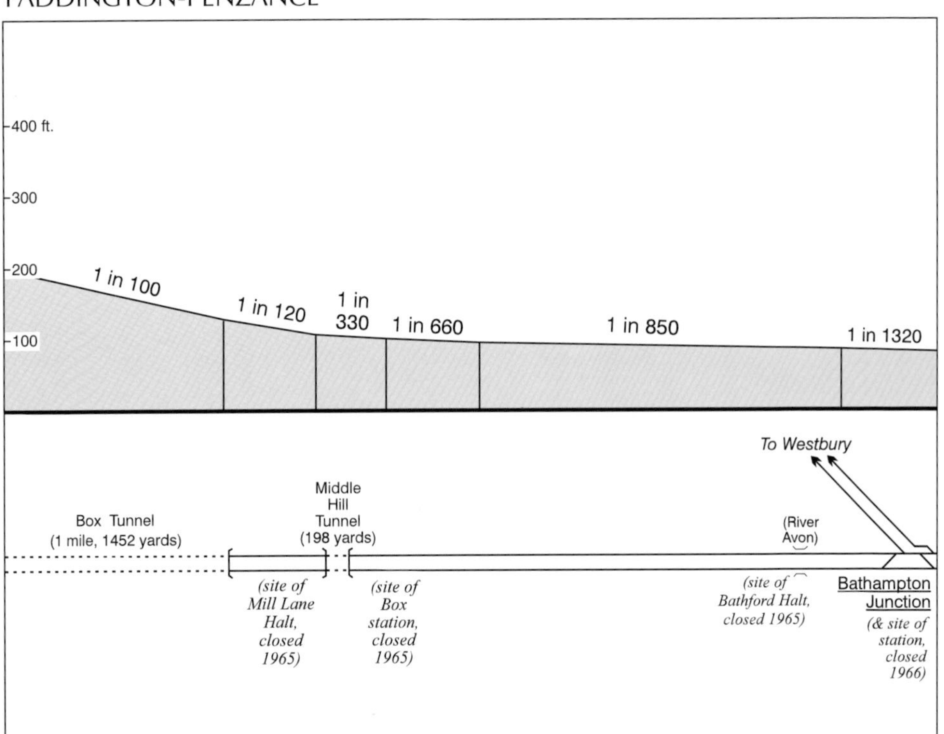

BOX TUNNEL : A vantage point by the side of the A4 road at Box affords a fine view of Brunel's famous tunnel, where a plaque records the occasion when the west portal was cleaned and restored by the Western Region in 1986 to commemorate its 150th anniversary. Box Tunnel was constructed between 1836-1841 to a length of 3,212 yards, from which an HST can be seen emerging from the west portal forming 1C52, the 1545 Paddington to Bristol Temple Meads. (MB 04/00)

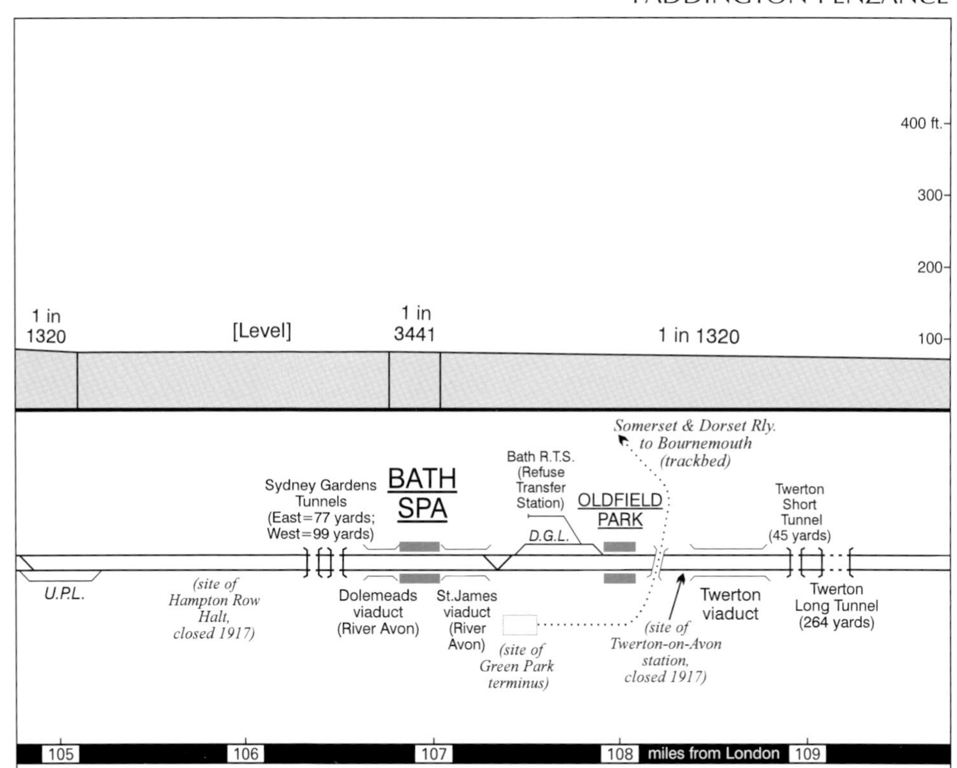

BATH SPA : Substituting for a HST (a shortage caused as a result of the 1999 Ladbroke Grove disaster), 47832 waits to leave Bath Spa with 1A29, the 0630 Plymouth to Paddington. Note the stripe on the class 47, applied by First Great Western to be in keeping with their HST fleet. (MB 04/00)

BATHAMPTON JUNCTION : The 1435 Cardiff to Warminster service, formed of class 153 unit No. 153377, is about to leave the main line at Bathampton Junction, from where it will proceed down the scenic Avon valley to Bradford on Avon. (MB 04/00)

BATH : The spa town of Bath is famous for its fine architecture, such as the Roman Baths, Royal Crescent and Abbey, the latter being a dominant feature in this excellent panoramic view of Bath, which sees large logo 37408 *Loch Rannoch* approaching the station with 2V70, the 0839 Weymouth to Bristol Temple Meads. (MG 08/97)

BOX MIDDLE TUNNEL : This is a popular location amongst railway photographers, where 58029 was recorded emerging from the west portal with the Avon 'Binliner'. (MG 06/95)

OLDFIELD PARK : Having deposited some containers in the Avon County Council waste terminal at Oldfield Park, Bath, 66024 waits to leave with the remaining containers for Bristol. (MB 08/00)

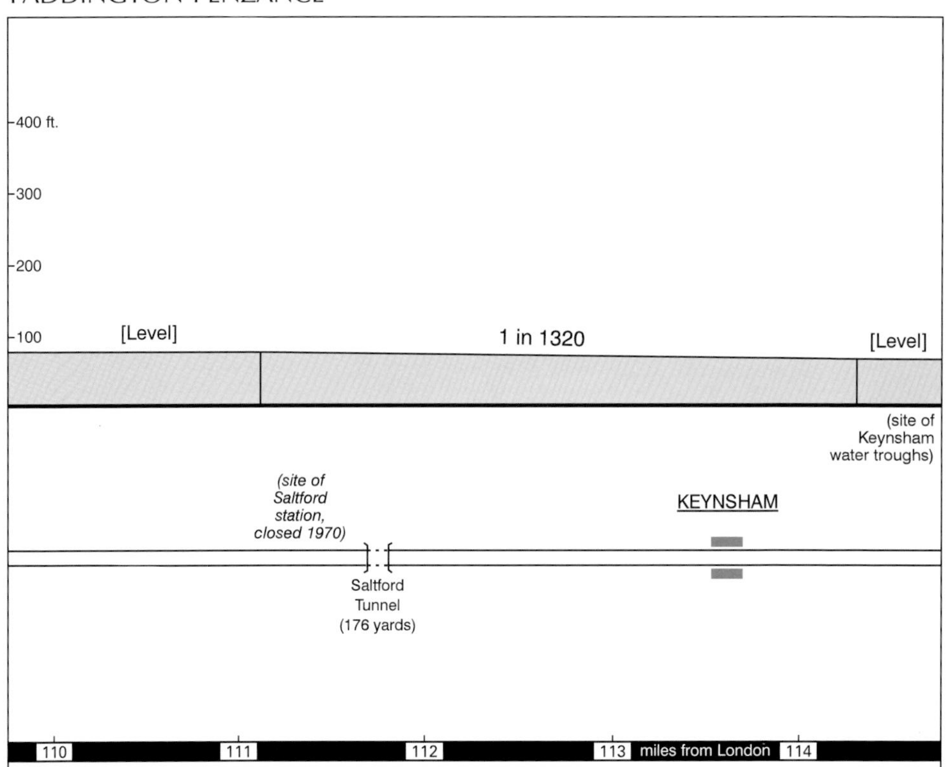

KEYNSHAM : *Wales & West* operated Class 37 hauled passenger services to Weymouth and were once a familiar sight on the main line between Bristol and Bathampton Junction. One such service, 2O86, the 0830 Bristol to Weymouth, is seen passing the site of Keynsham water troughs, behind 37427 *Highland Enterprise*. (MG 07/98)

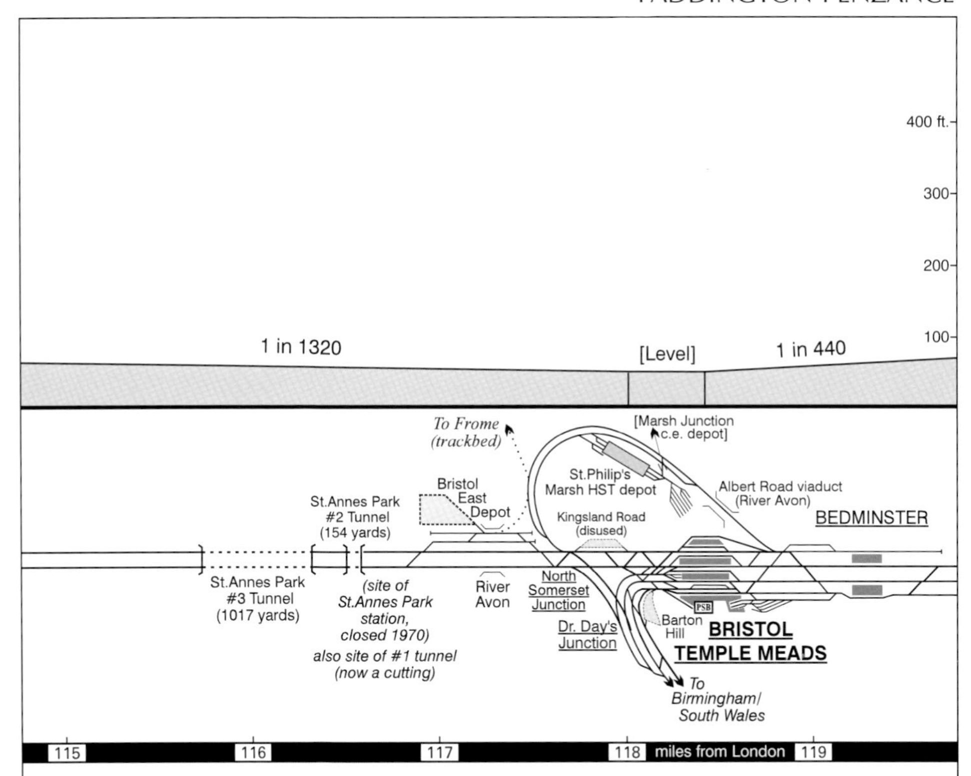

BRISTOL EAST DEPOT : The sidings at Bristol East Depot are used to stable engineers trains, as can be seen in this view of 'push/pull' class 33/1 locomotive No. 33116, passing with a Waterloo to Weymouth railtour. Although working a railtour on this occasion, the class used to regularly work passenger services between Bristol/Cardiff and Portsmouth Harbour. (RD 01/94)

NORTH SOMERSET JUNCTION : The 'Avon Binliner' heads across the River Avon at North Somerset Junction behind 37800 with containers which will be loaded with household refuse at Barrow Road and Stoke Gifford, thence to the landfill site at Calvert, near Bicester. (MG 06/98)

KINGSLAND ROAD : The City of Bristol skyline provides an impressive backdrop as an unidentified class 47 hauls 5081, the 0947 Bristol Temple Meads to Tonbridge empty mail vans, past some old GUV, BG and Mark 1 vehicles stabled in the sidings at Kingsland Road. Behind the train, further vans can be seen outside Barton Hill maintenance depot. (RD 07/96)

BRISTOL TEMPLE MEADS : A bird's eye view shows the layout and impressive overall canopy roof at Temple Meads station as an HST leaves with 1V41, the 0645 Newcastle to Plymouth. Since this picture was taken, the tracks leading to both sides of the platform on the extreme right-hand side of the picture have been fully restored for use by *Virgin's* Voyager trains in 2002. (MB 04/00)

Looking back towards Temple Meads, 47817 (below) hauls 1V36, the 0614 Preston to Paignton under Bath Road bridge formed of DVT 82102 and a set of Mark 2 coaches. (MG 08/98)

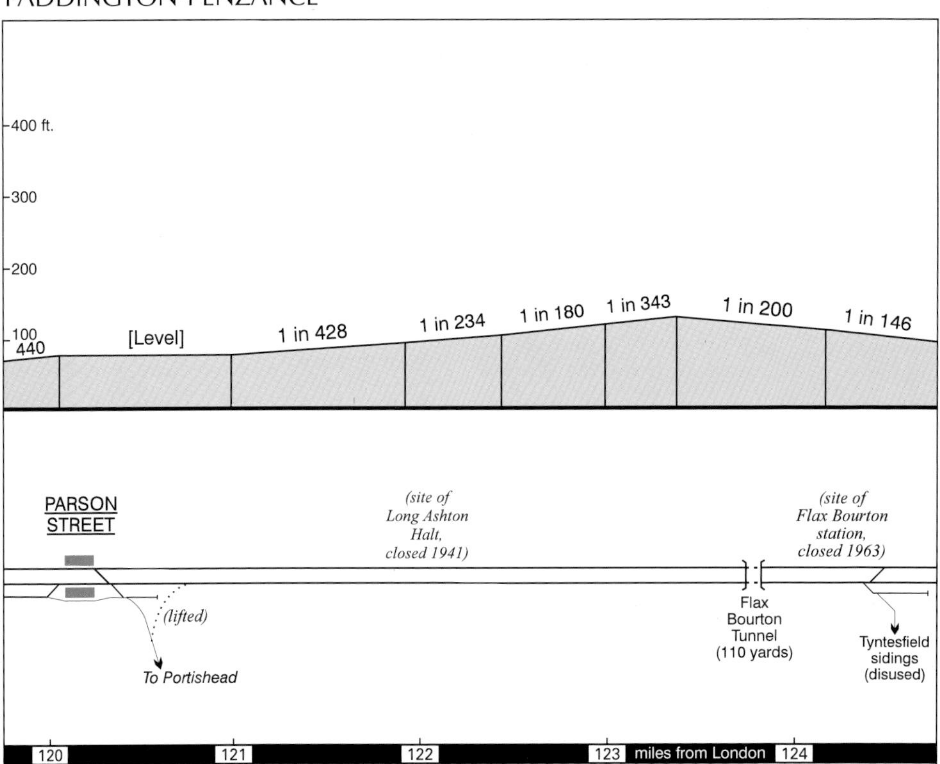

FLAX BOURTON : Situated between Nailsea & Blackwell and Parson Street; Flax Bourton is the location for 43098 *railway children* as it heads the "Devonian" (1E31, 0821 Paignton to Newcastle) over the crossover which lead to disused sidings. (RG 06/98)

400 ft.
300
200
100

1 in 387 | 1 in 334 | 1 in 471 | 1 in 545 | [Level]

NAILSEA & BACKWELL

125 | 126 | 127 | 128 miles from London | 129

NAILSEA & BACKWELL : Looking from the station footbridge, 47738 *Bristol Barton Hill* hauls 4 vans through Nailsea & Backwell forming 1C53, the 1602 Paddington to Plymouth mail. (RG 06/95)

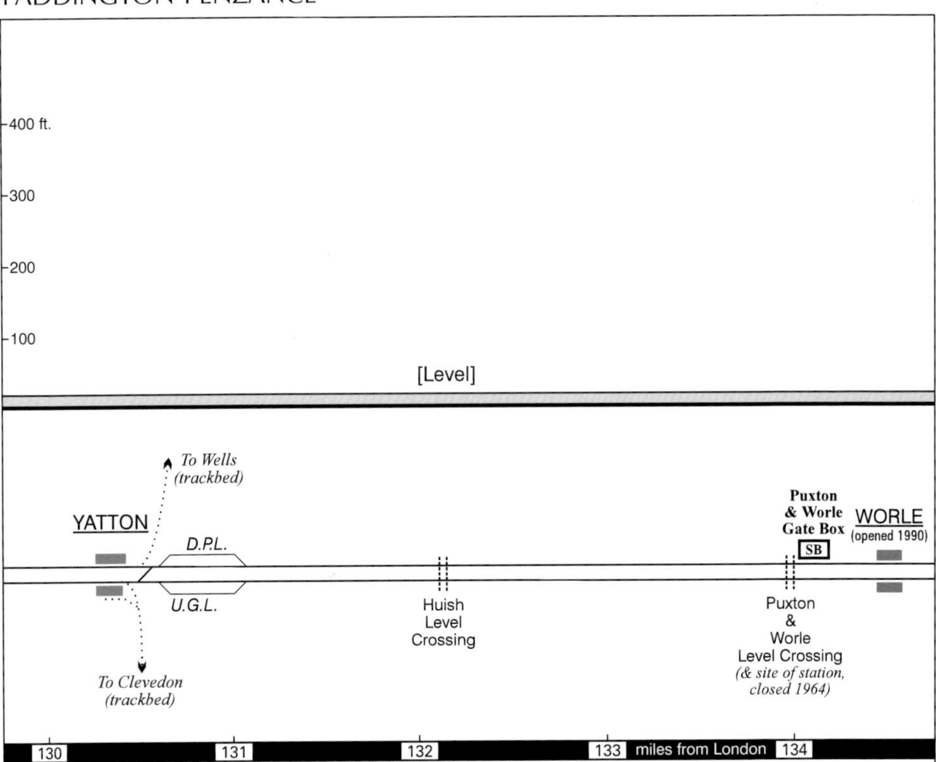

YATTON : With Yatton station visible in the distance, 60065 *Kinder Low* slows to enter the down goods loop in charge of 6V70, the 0857 Cliffe Vale to St. Blazey 'Enterprise' service. Note the touched up paintwork and incomplete locomotive number on the front of the class 60. (RG 09/96)

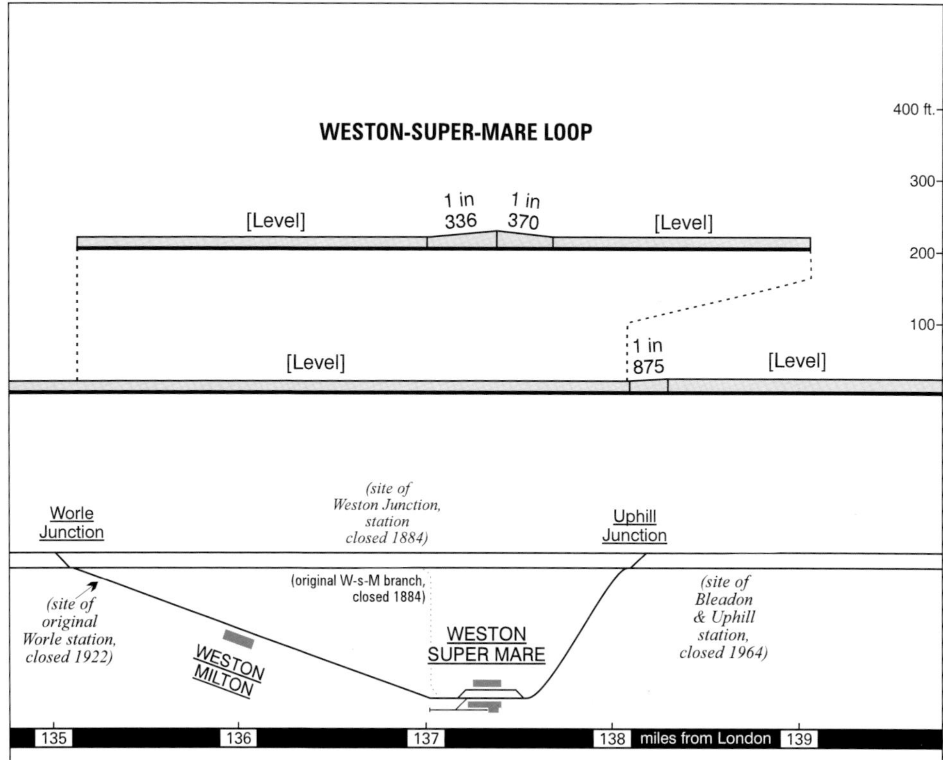

WORLE JUNCTION : The single line loop which serves Weston-super-Mare leaves the main line at Worle Junction and rejoins nearly 4 miles later at Uphill Junction. At Worle Junction, 43002/43139 are seen in charge of 1A34, the 0730 Plymouth to Paddington. (RG 04/00)

WESTON-SUPER-MARE : The area taken up by the car park in this view used to be the site of the locomotive stabling sidings and turntable. *Porterbrook* liveried 47817 (above) is leaving Weston-super-Mare on 1M56, the 1033 Paignton to Manchester, passing under Hildesheim bridge, named to commemorate Weston-super-Mare's link with Hildesheim, Germany. (RG 06/96)

A busy scene at Weston-super-Mare as 43098 *railway children* (below) prepares to lead the 'Devonian' out of the station, whilst 150233 waits with the 1000 departure to Bristol Temple Meads. A Railtrack 'Stoneblower' machine is stabled in the bay platform. (RG 04/00)

400 ft.
300
200
100

924 712

[Level]

(site of Brean Road Halt, closed 1955)

(site of Brent Knoll Halt, closed 1971)

140 141 142 143 miles from London 144

BRENT KNOLL : A delightful setting at Brent Knoll for 37673+37669 heading 6C20, the 1350 Newport ADJ to St. Blazey 'Enterprise' service, whose main payload on this occasion was coal. The area around the footbridge in the background is the site of Brent Knoll station. (RG 05/97)

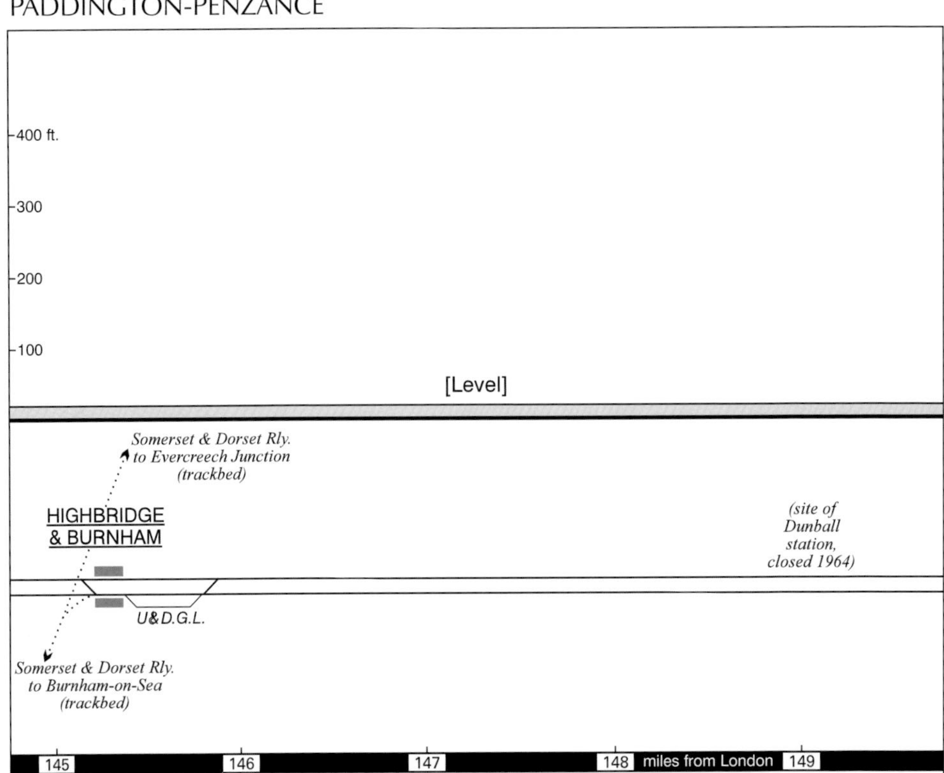

HIGHBRIDGE : The "Cornishman" passes through Highbridge station with leading power car 43155 *City of Aberdeen* the only vehicle in the train set sporting *Virgin Trains* corporate livery. (RG 09/97)

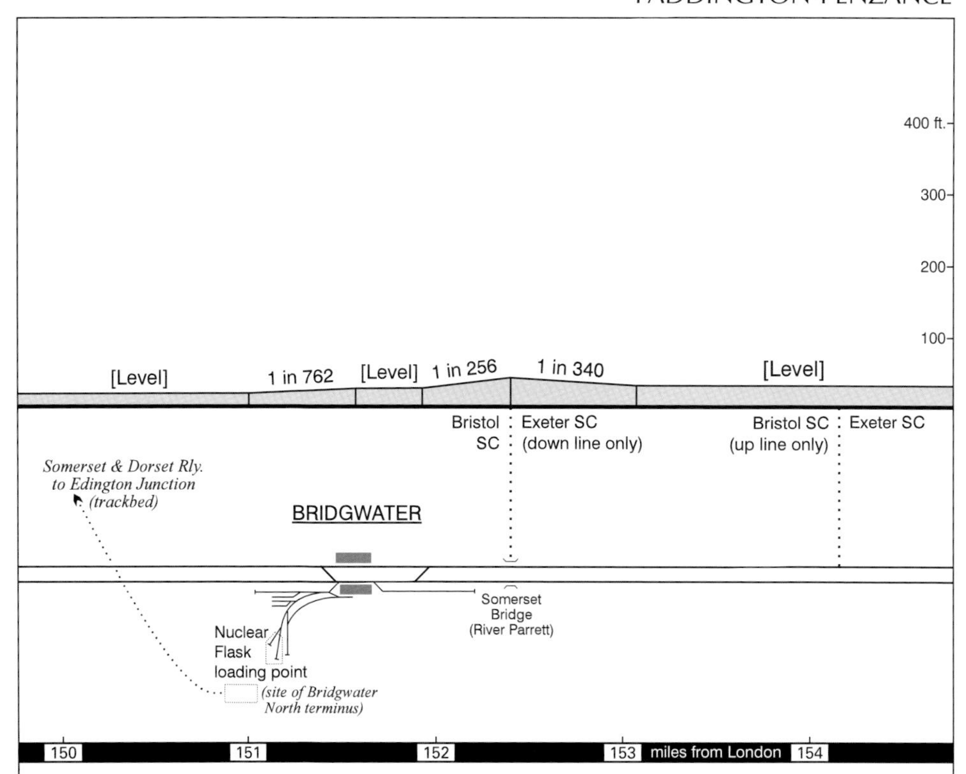

BRIDGWATER : The sidings on the north side of the main line at Bridgwater station are used to transfer nuclear flasks arriving by road from Hinkley Point power station to wagons for a weekly rail journey to the Sellafield reprocessing plant. In this view, 56069 *Wolverhampton Steel Terminal* shunts some wagons in readiness for 7M53, the 1427 departure to Sellafield. This was the last train run under EWS operation before control was transferred to Direct Rail Services. (RG 02/99)

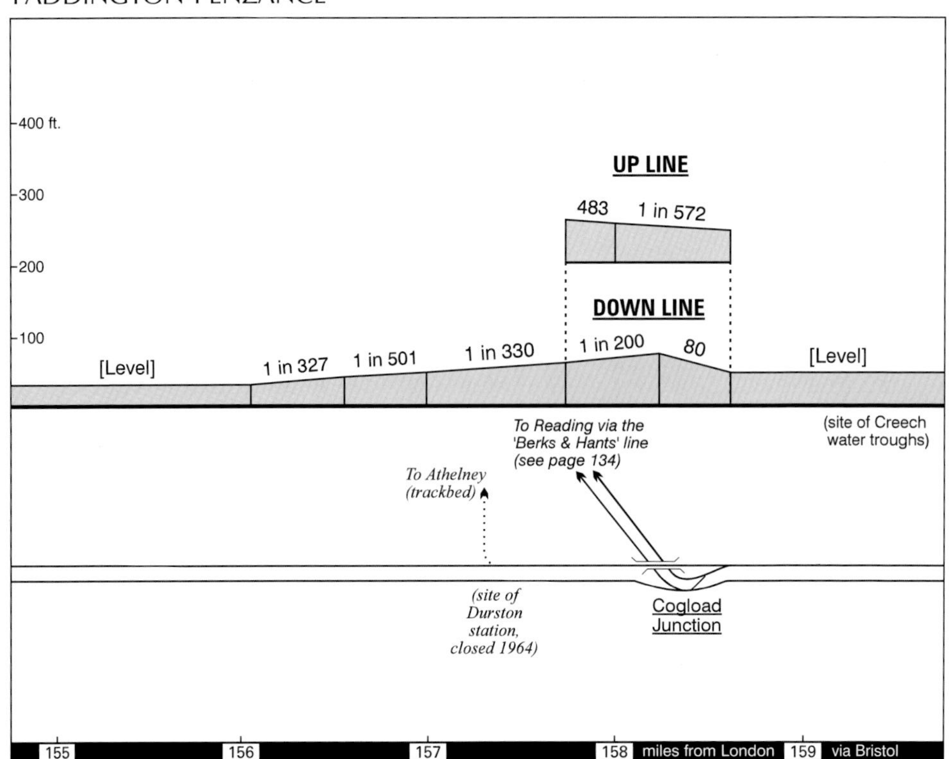

COGLOAD : An HST (43125/43012) proceeds along the up main line near Cogload with the 0548 service from Plymouth to London Paddington. The 'Berks & Hants' joins up with the Great Western Main Line at Cogload Junction and the flyover can be seen in the background, which takes the down main line over the 'Berks. & Hants.' (SM 06/93)

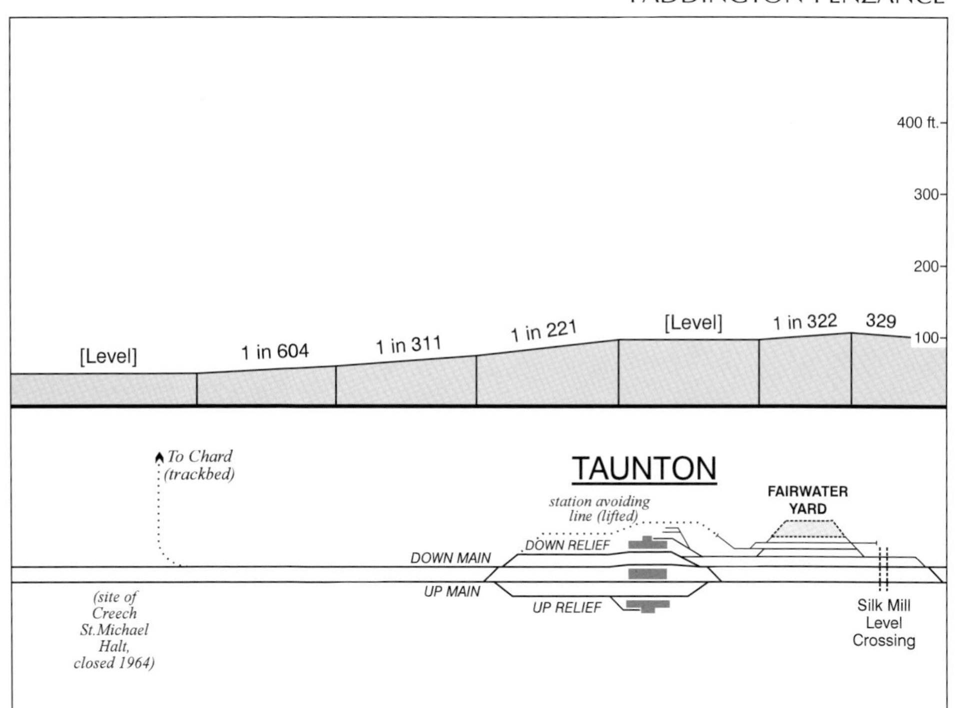

TAUNTON : A Paddington bound HST awaits departure as 60021 *Pen-y-Ghent* passes through Taunton station with 6V70, the 0857 Cliffe Vale to St. Blazey china clay empties. Note the former GWR corrugated metal and brick goods shed to the right of the picture. (DM 03/00)

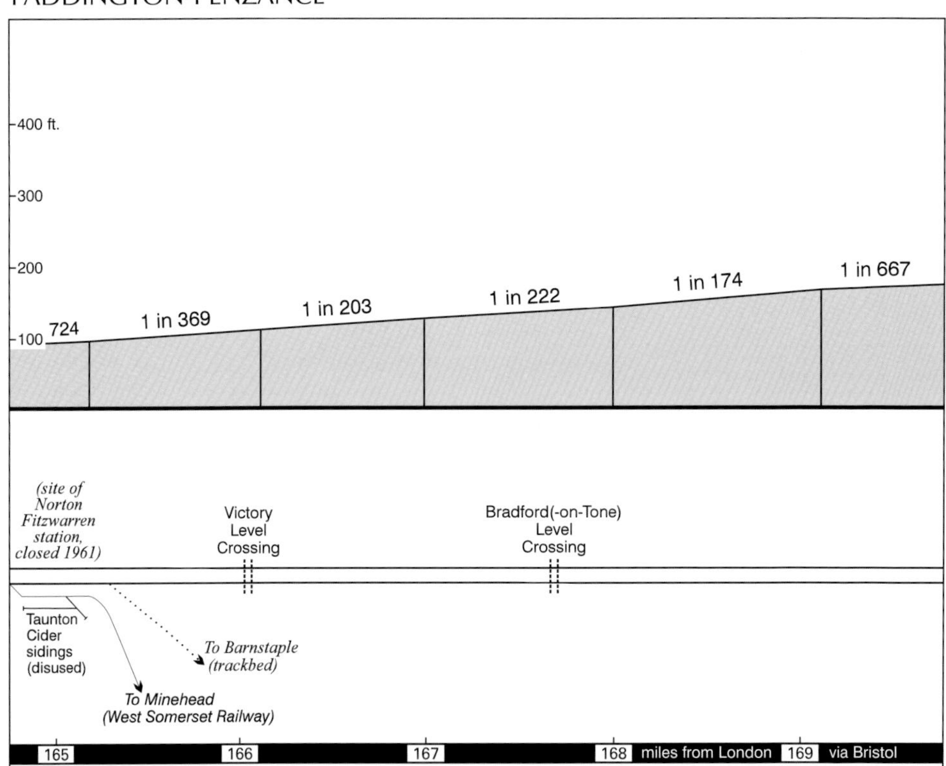

NORTON FITZWARREN : The West Somerset Railway has a connection to the main line at Norton Fitzwarren where 60043 passes with 6B68, the 0940 Burngullow to Newport ADJ china clay tanks. It was at Norton Fitzwarren in 1940 when the Paddington to Penzance sleeper, hauled by steam locomotive 6028 *King George VI*, derailed on catch points and resulted in 28 fatalities. (DM 03/00)

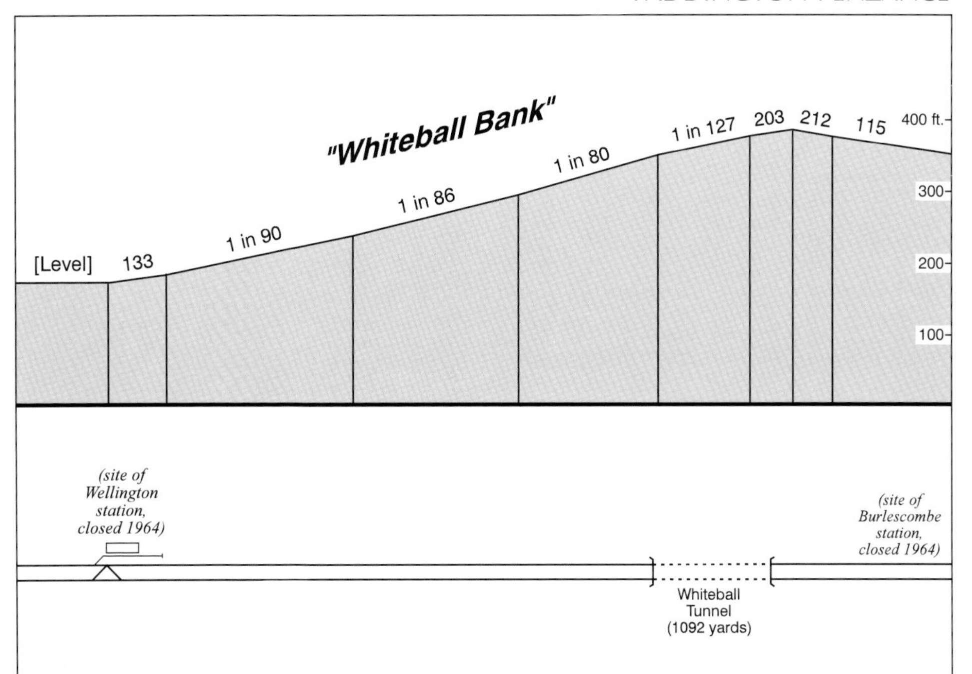

BURLESCOMBE : Near the village of Burlescombe, 47812 works hard against the grade on the climb to Whiteball Summit with 1M56, the 0848 Penzance to Manchester, whose train formation comprises a rake of *Virgin* liveried Mark 2 air-conditioned coaches. (DM 08/99)

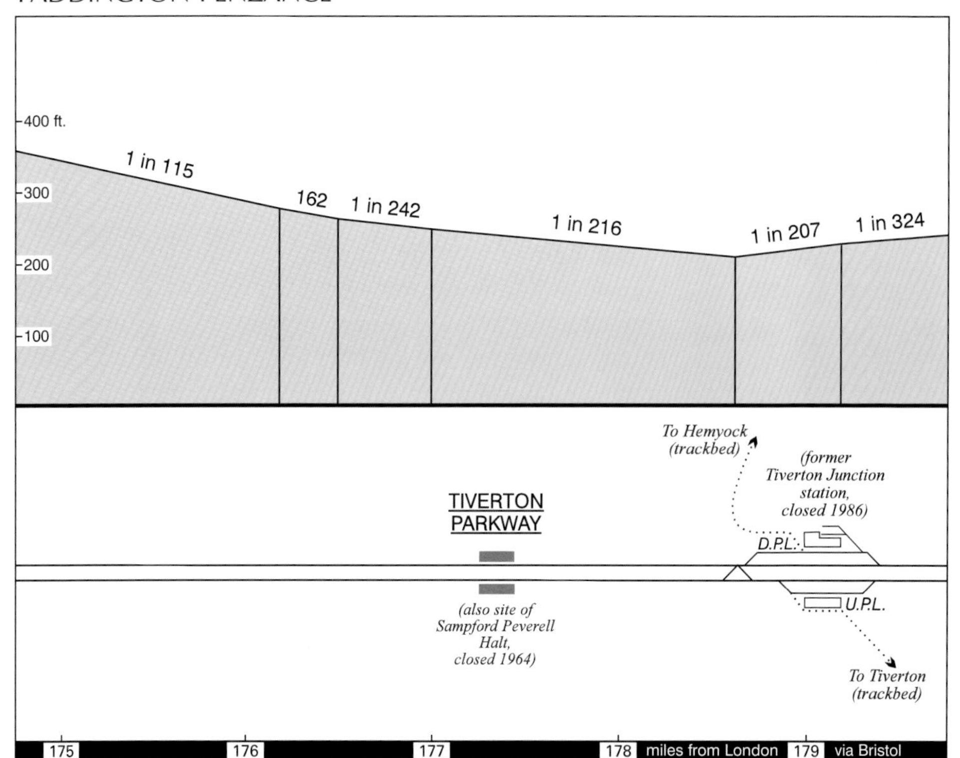

TIVERTON PARKWAY : Like Bodmin, Tiverton is another station which is remote from the town. In fact, to develop greater accessibility, a 'park & ride' scheme was introduced at a new Tiverton Parkway station, which resulted in the old Tiverton Junction station closing. At the new Parkway, an HST passes through with the northbound "Cornish Scot". (DM 05/99)

400 ft.
300
200
100

1 in 155 | 1 in 316 | 279 | 212 | 1 in 333 | 1 in 824 | 1 in 306 | 1 in 523

(site of Cullompton station, closed 1964)

180 | 181 | 182 | 183 miles from London | 184

WILLAND : The site of Tiverton Junction station (see diagram opposite) is situated behind the bridge in this photograph of 66087 heading a ballast train from Westbury to Exeter Riverside. (DM 05/99)

400 ft.
300
200
100

1 in 292 | 1 in 313 | 1 in 219 | 1 in 243 | 1 in 435 | 1 in 343 | 1 in 500 | 271 | 1 in 217

(site of Silverton station, closed 1964)

Hele & Bradnich Level Crossing *(& site of station, closed 1964)*

185 | 186 | 187 | 188 miles from London | 189 via Bristol

SILVERTON : Booked for a pair of class 37 locomotives at the time; 7C28, the 1106 Exeter to Merehead empty box stone wagons approaches the site of Silverton station behind 58047, a class of locomotive not commonly seen in this part of the country. (DM 09/99)

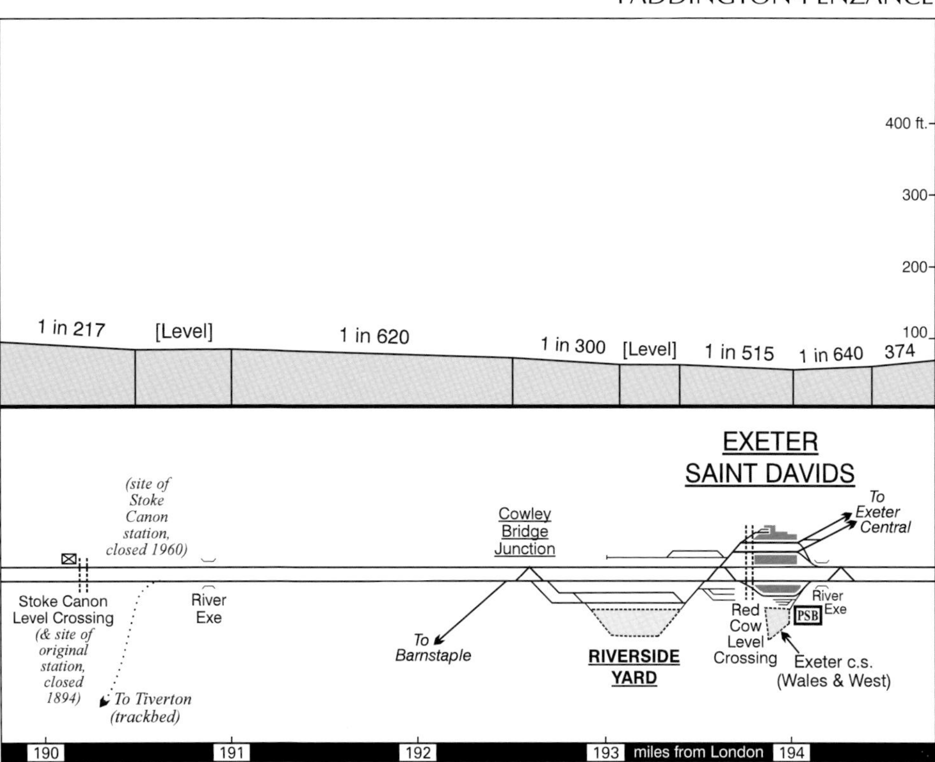

COWLEY BRIDGE JUNCTION : Cowley Bridge, where the Barnstaple branch joins the main line, is a favourite location for photographers and is situated in an area notorious for flooding from the adjacent River Exe. As it rounds the curve, 60040 passes the mock Tudor style inn with 6C21, the 1451 Newport ADJ to St. Blazey 'Enterprise'. (DM 06/99)

EXETER RIVERSIDE : The yard at Exeter Riverside is an important staging point for freight traffic travelling to/from the west country. In the yard, 66188 heads a rake of ballast empties bound for Westbury and 60071 *Dorothy Garrod* is on 6M72, the 1655 St. Blazey to Cliffe Vale. (DM 03/00)

EXETER CARRIAGE SIDINGS : The carriage sidings and fuel point are situated on the up side of the main line adjacent to Exeter St. Davids station. Early one Sunday morning in late Spring, when the fog was slow to clear, a line up of units could be seen stabled, which were from left to right: 150254/158838/153368/150253/150238/153377/150239/153353. (MB 05/00)

EXETER ST DAVIDS : This is the most important of the three stations in Exeter (the others being Central and St. Thomas) and is a major interchange station for services to Barnstaple, Exmouth and stations on the former Southern Region line to Salisbury. The distinct towers housing the lift shafts rise from the platforms either side of an HST (above) which is ready to leave Exeter St. Davids bound for Paddington. (MB 07/00)

A manually patrolled level crossing still operates at the east end of the station where 47846 *Thor* (below) is seen crossing the road with a Motorail service from Paddington to Penzance. (MB 07/00)

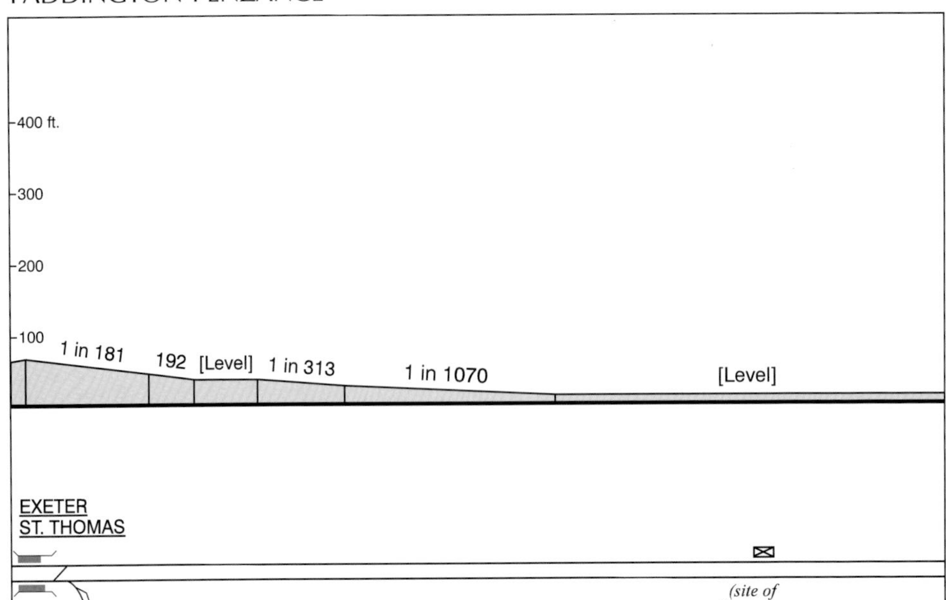

EXMINSTER : The leading power car (43130) has a slightly different livery to that of the coaches which make up 1A71, the 1445 Paignton to Paddington *First Great Western* train service, as it passes the redundant but well preserved signalbox at Exminster. (DM 09/99)

400 ft.
300
200
100

[Level] 258 [Level] 409 [L] 377

(site of Exminster water troughs)

STARCROSS

DAWLISH WARREN

200 201 202 203 miles from London 204

DAWLISH WARREN : The Exe Estuary is in the background in this view of 150234 leaving Dawlish Warren with a local service from Exmouth to Paignton. Of note are the old GWR chocolate & cream coaches, now used as holiday accommodation. (DM 03/00)

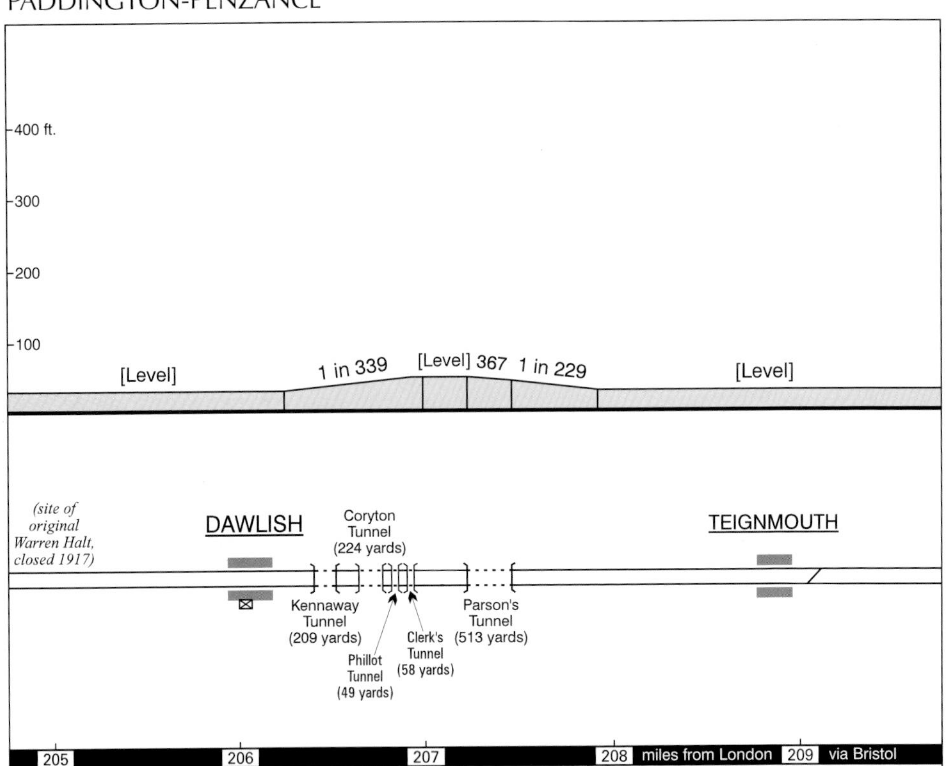

DAWLISH : Running over one hour late, *Fragonset* liveried 47709 makes its way after the Dawlish station stop in charge of 1M56, the 0848 Penzance to Manchester. Of note is the elevated, but now boarded up, signalbox on the up platform and Kennaway Tunnel visible in the background. (MB 05/00)

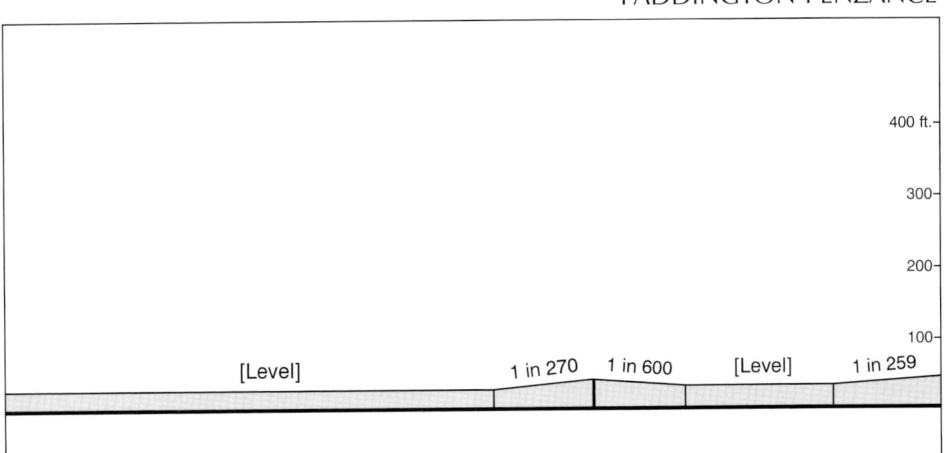

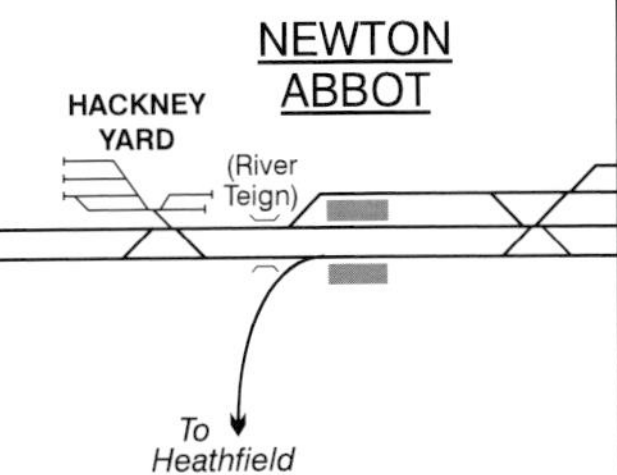

210 211 212 213 miles from London 214

NEWTON ABBOT : *South West Trains* turbo 159007, resplendent in *Stagecoach* colours, leaves Newton Abbot with the 1035 service from London Waterloo to Paignton. To the right of the train is the site of the former carriage sidings and diesel maintenance depot. (DM 03/00)

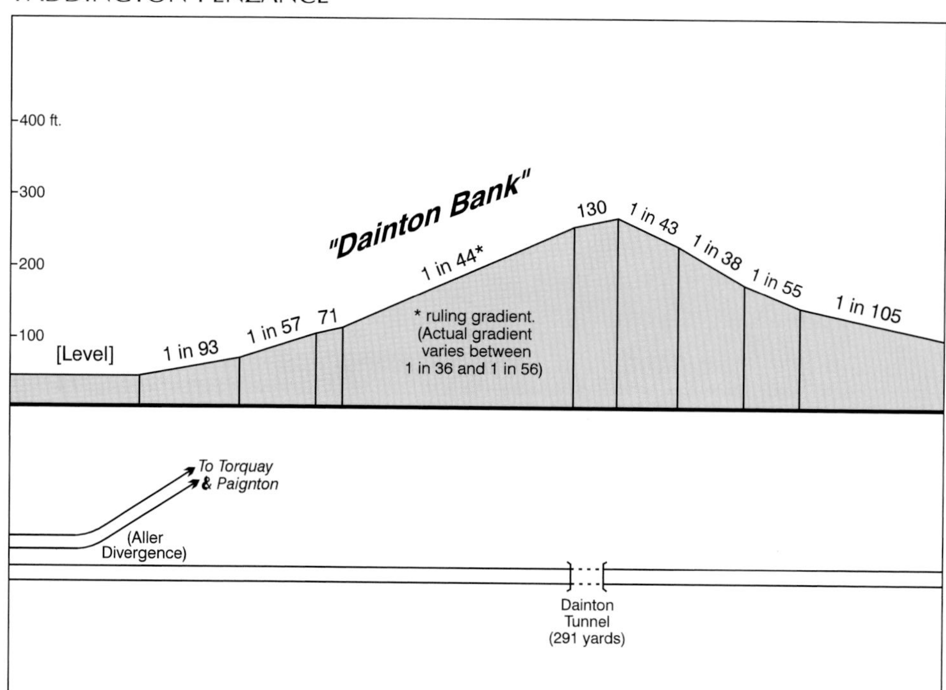

DAINTON : After a 2½ mile climb from Aller, the main line reaches Dainton summit and tunnel, where 37220 is seen having emerged from the tunnel's west portal with a train of short wheel-base oil tanks bound for Tavistock Junction. (RW 07/92)

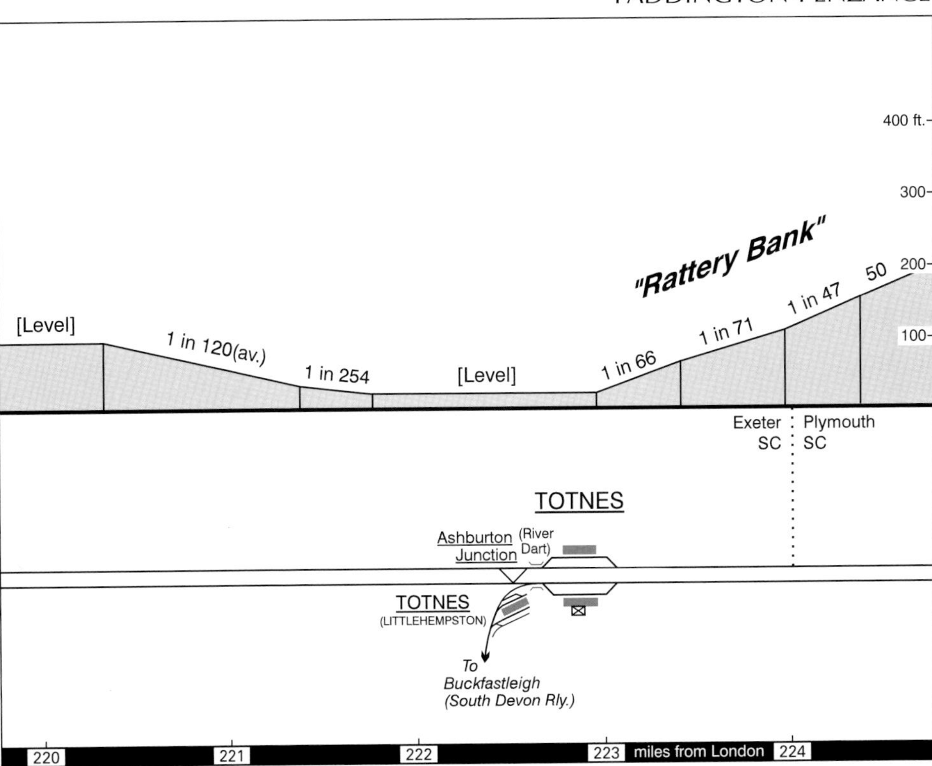

TOTNES : A plume of smoke issues from 43023 as the up "Cornish Riviera" accelerates through Totnes. The station's architecture is of interest, particularly the former signalbox which is preserved as the station buffet; alas, the former GWR overbridge built in 1888 has long gone. (MB 07/00)

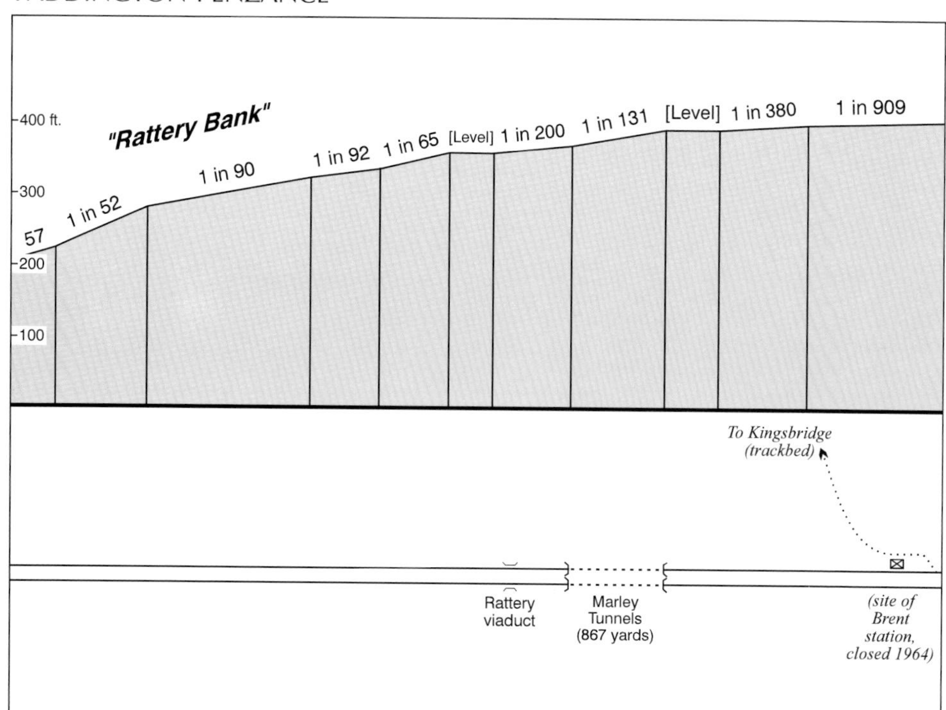

RATTERY : After leaving Totnes, the main line begins the severe climb up 'Rattery Bank' until the summit is eventually reached at Wrangaton, 455 feet above sea level. Transrail liveried 60096 *Ben Macdui* is seen at Rattery in charge of 6V70, the 0857 Cliffe Vale to St. Blazey service. (RW 06/96)

1 in 243 | 400 | 129 | 1 in 117 | 1 in 307 | [Level] | 1 in 122 | 1 in 295 | 218 | 1 in 150

400 ft.
300
200
100

Wrangaton summit,
455 feet above sea level
(highest point between
Paddington & Penzance)

Glazebrook viaduct

Bittaford viaduct

IVYBRIDGE
(opened 1994)

Aish crossovers

(site of Wrangaton station, closed 1959)

(site of Bittaford Halt, closed 1959)

230 | 231 | 232 | 233 miles from London | 234

SOUTH BRENT : On the fringe of Dartmoor, 37521+37696 pass the old signalbox and site of Brent station (see diagram opposite) at the helm of 6C43, 1248 St. Blazey to Exeter Riverside 'Enterprise'. Brent station, until its closure in 1964, used to provide a local service to Kingsbridge. (RW 06/96)

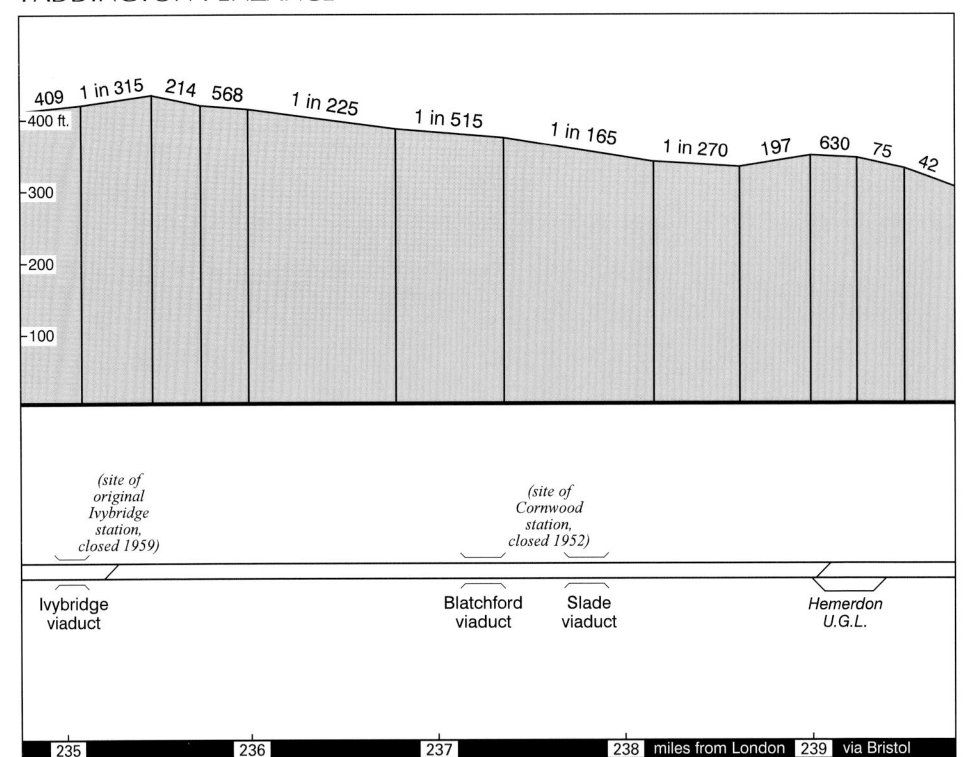

BLATCHFORD VIADUCT : A weekend ECS from Laira to Paignton is seen behind 47805 heading east over the viaduct situated in a beautiful wooded area near Cornwood. Of note are the two piers of an earlier structure visible in front of the present viaduct. (RW 05/97)

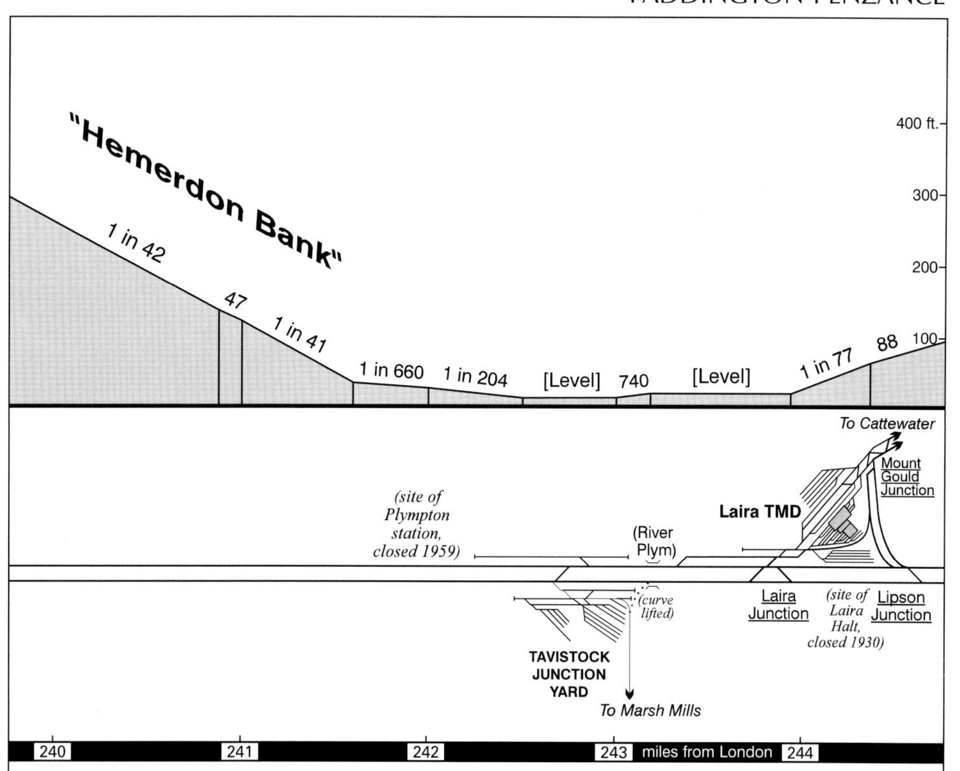

TAVISTOCK JUNCTION : The yard at Tavistock Junction lies to the east of the A38 flyover (visible in the background) and handles mainly departmental traffic along with china clay wagons from Marsh Mills. In this view, 37673 reverses empty CDA china clay wagons into the yard. (DM 08/98)

LAIRA JUNCTION : This elevated view from the A374 road shows 158871 heading alongside the River Plym at Laira Junction, two miles from Plymouth, with a Bristol to Penzance service. (DM 10/97)

LAIRA : A solitary class 47 can be seen stabled at Laira maintenance depot, which services a fleet of *First Great Western* and *Virgin Trains* HSTs. The lines leading to the servicing bays are clearly visible plus the Great Western main line sweeping away to the right of the picture. (MB 07/00)

PLYMOUTH : This photograph shows the layout to the east of Plymouth station as 47845 *County of Kent* leaves with 1M56, the 0846 Penzance to Manchester; a view dominated by a multi- storey office block above Plymouth station; note 37516 and mail vans stabled. (MB 07/00)

KEYHAM : The unloading is well underway as 59103 *Village of Mells* waits in a siding adjacent to Keyham station for the return leg of its journey back to the Mendips, having arrived with a special train of aggregate from Whatley Quarry. (DM 11/98)

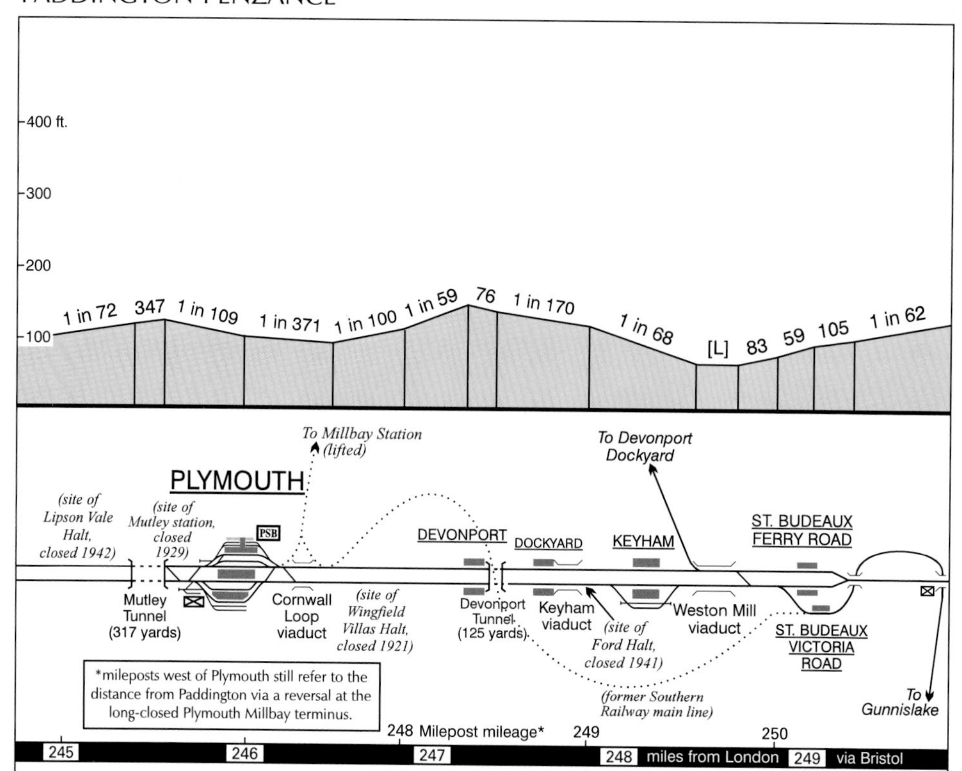

ROYAL ALBERT BRIDGE : The River Tamar is a natural boundary between Devon and Cornwall, spanned by two magnificent bridges. The dedication "I. K. Brunel, Engineer, 1859" can be seen on the east portal of the Royal Albert railway bridge, which 37667+37668 have crossed with 6M72, the 1655 St. Blazey to Cliffe Vale loaded china clay tanks. On the right is the Tamar road bridge. (DM 09/99)

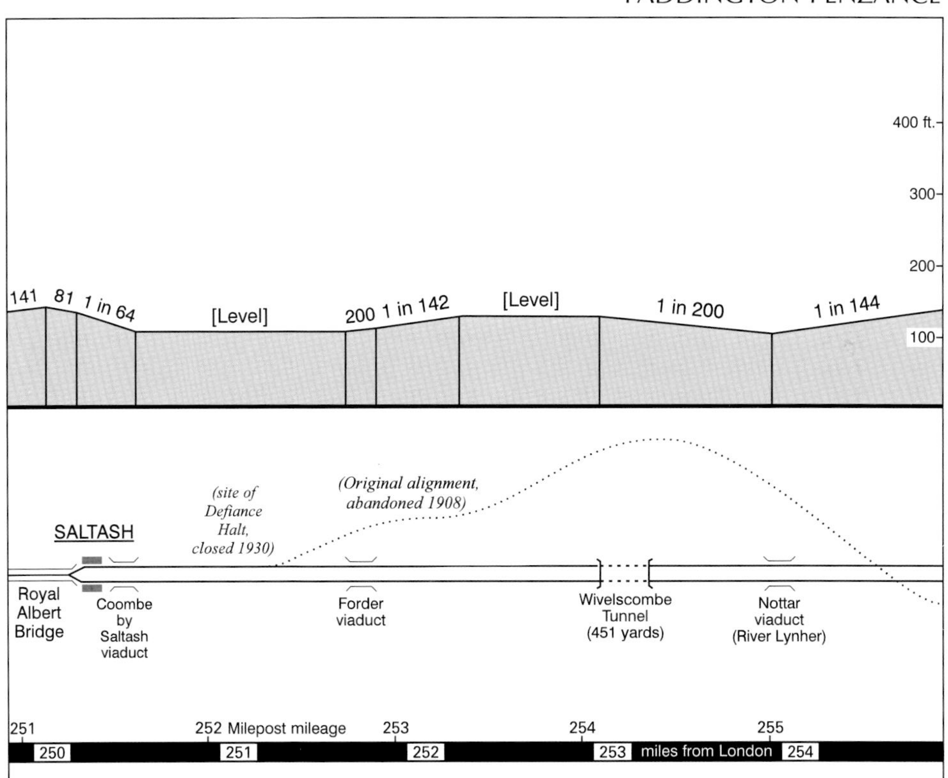

SALTASH : The western pier of the Tamar road bridge overshadows 158867 as it passes through Saltash station and into Cornwall with a Manchester to Penzance service. (DM 05/99)

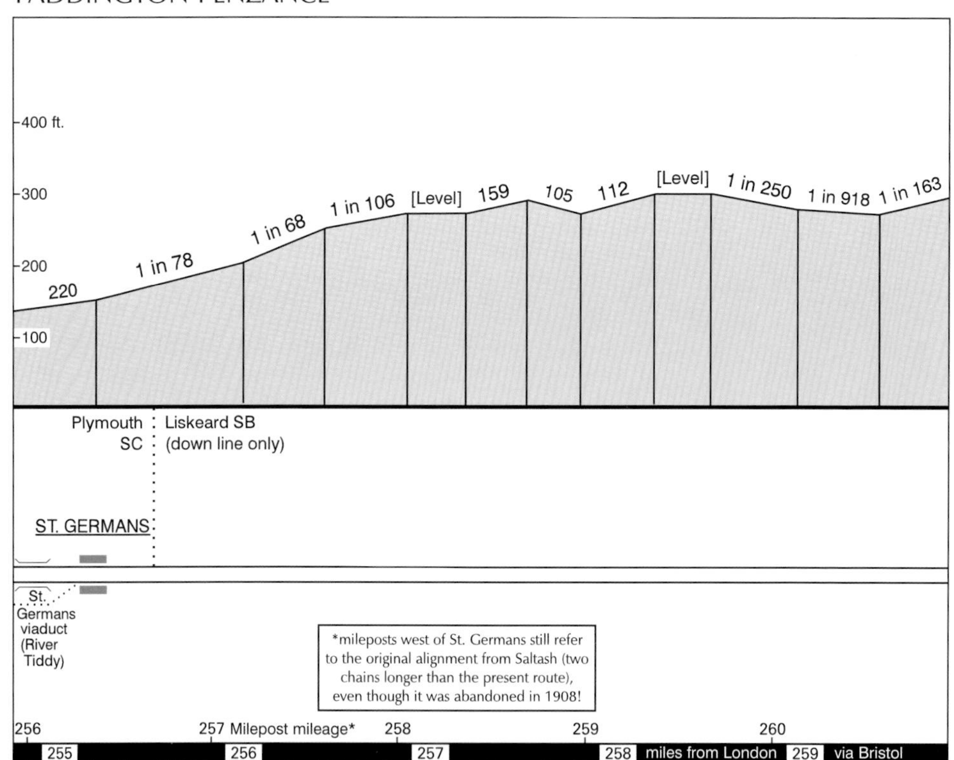

ST. GERMANS : Threatening storm clouds gather overhead as a Class 158 unit passes the well kept, whitewashed, station building at St. Germans with a Penzance to Cardiff service. (MB 10/00)

TRERULEFOOT : Perhaps, a somewhat unremarkable photograph of a 'sprinter' forming a Penzance to Paignton service, seen at Trerulefoot between St. Germans and Menheniot. However, many readers may consider the sight of snow in Cornwall rather more remarkable! Although this was the worst snow in the county since 1987, by three o'clock in the afternoon it had all melted. (RW 02/94)

BOLITHO : One of the longest freight flows on the railway network is 6S55, the 0940 Burngullow to Irvine, which conveys china clay slurry to Ayrshire in Scotland. The train is seen on the outskirts of Liskeard, having crossed Bolitho viaduct, with 60075 at the head running over 5 hours late! Of note is the semaphore signal, a foretaste of signalling as we trace the route deeper into Cornwall. (RW 10/99)

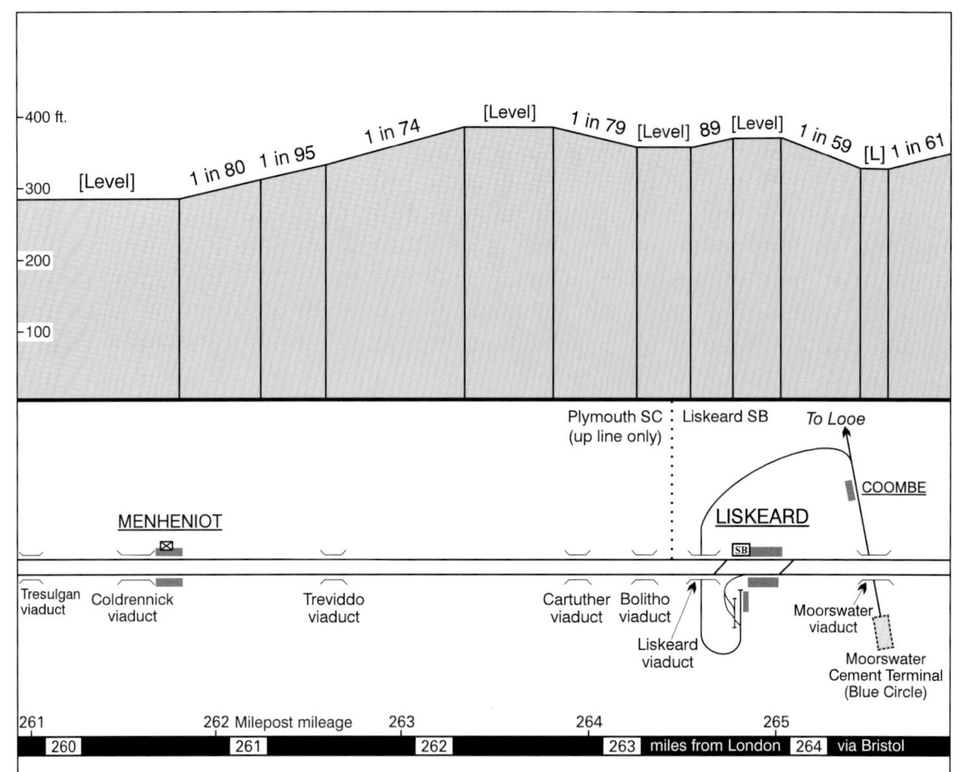

LISKEARD : The station area at Liskeard is controlled by a manual signalbox and semaphore signals, which can be seen in this view of 37668 bringing 6C91, the 1300 Moorswater to St. Blazey, empty cargowagons into Liskeard station. (DM 07/99)

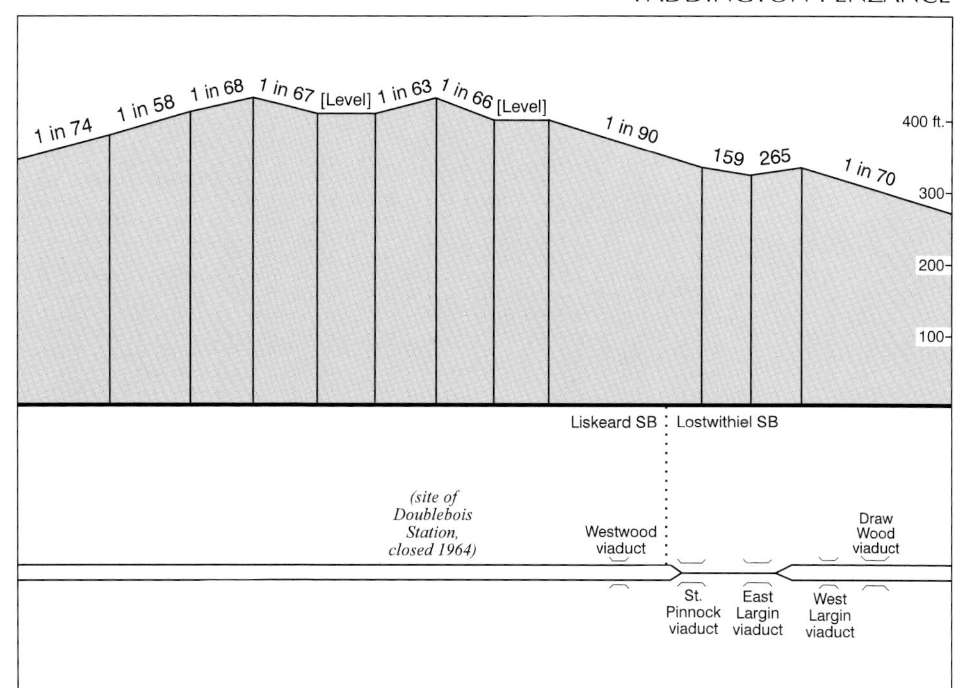

LARGIN : A shortage of stock resulted in *Virgin Cross Country* hiring train sets from other Train Operating Companies to fulfil their summer (Saturday) timetable services in 1998. One such service, 1V38, the 0605 Leeds to Newquay, employed a *Midland Mainline* HST set and this is seen crossing Largin East viaduct, with power car 43058 leading. (MG 07/98)

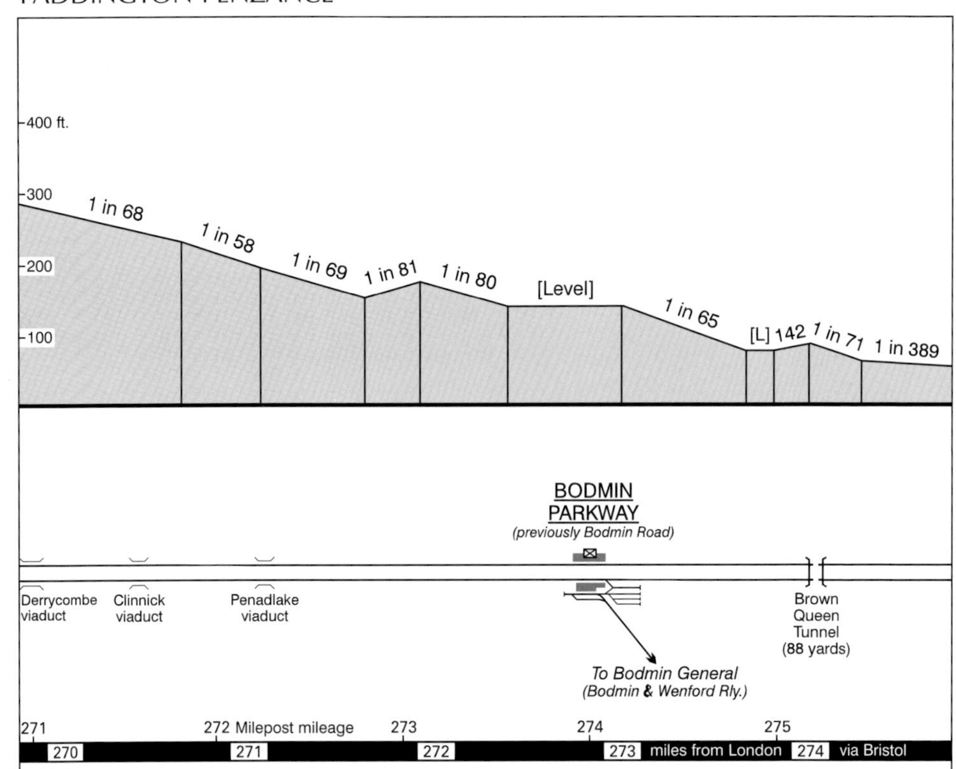

BODMIN PARKWAY : A bus service provides a link between the railway station and Bodmin, which is situated just under 4 miles away, now there is no longer a direct passenger service to the town. There is plenty of interest in this picture, namely the preserved signalbox and GWR footbridge, albeit the latter is in a rather forlorn state. It would also appear that a weed killing train is long overdue as 158865 crosses a well cultivated patch on its way to Penzance. (MB 07/00)

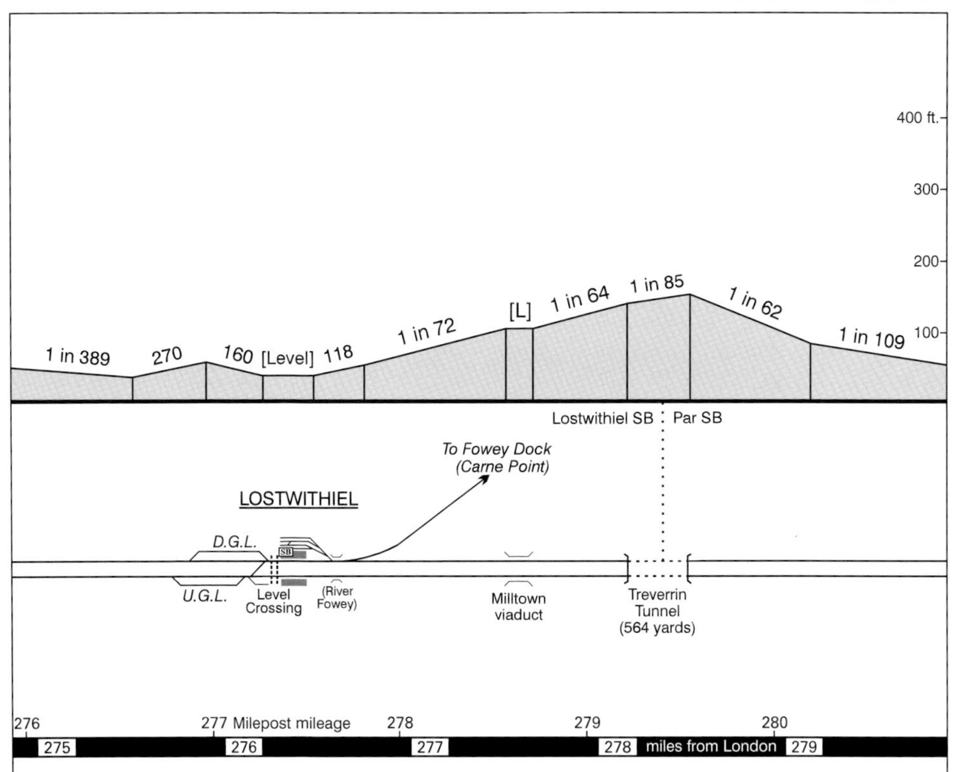

LOSTWITHIEL : Semaphores and signalboxes abound in Cornwall and examples of both are well illustrated here at Lostwithiel as 47845 *County of Kent* passes over the level crossing at the east end of the station heading 1V50, the 0840 service from Glasgow Central to Penzance. (MB 07/00)

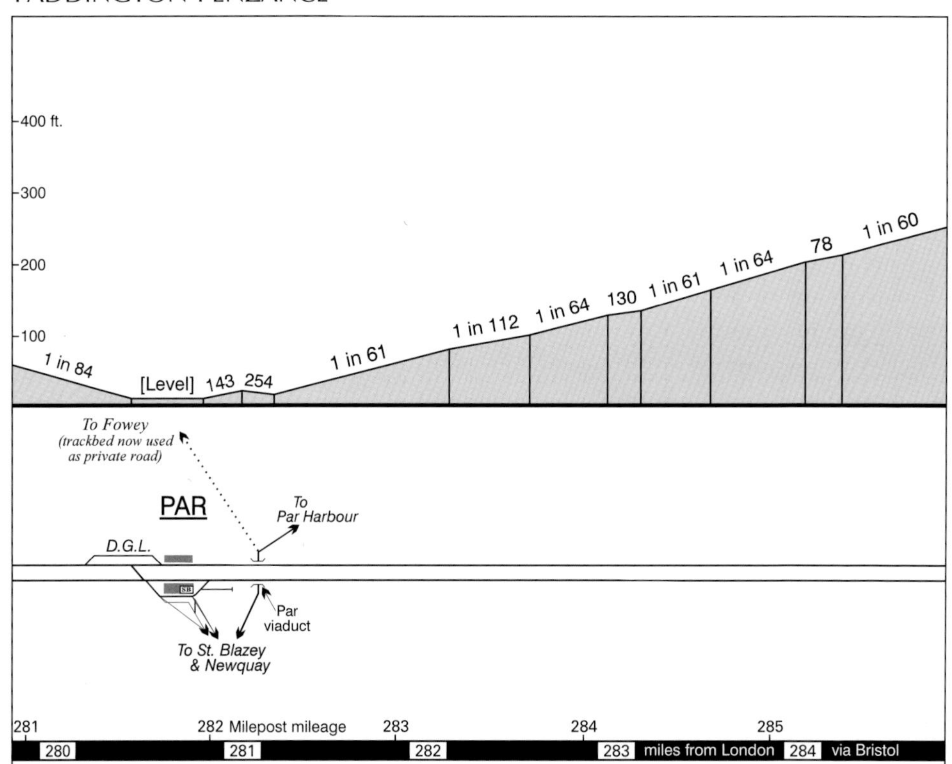

PAR : A rake of empty CDA china clay wagons from Fowey has been left in the down goods loop at Par by 66111, which is seen leaving for St Blazey depot; a second class 66 locomotive (66121) took the train forward an hour later. (MB 07/00)

PAR : The station layout is illustrated in this view, especially the island platform, the nearside of which is used by passenger trains serving Newquay. 67003 (above) leaves Par with 5M99, the 1808 St. Blazey to Plymouth empty TPO stock. (MB 07/00)

The signalbox and semaphores are predominant in this photograph of an HST (below) about to pass through Par station 'non-stop' with 1S71, the 0719 Penzance to Glasgow "Cornish Scot". (MB 07/00)

BURNGULLOW : The Blackpool clay dries dominate these two photographs of class 37's on local 'trips' at Burngullow. Transrail liveried 37674 *St. Blaise Church* 1445-1995 (above) leaves Burngullow with a train of china clay from Crugwallins bound for export at Carne Point, Fowey. (BA 11/97)

In the distance, 37521 waits for 37670 *St. Blazey T&RS Depot* (below) to come off the china clay branch at Burngullow Junction with CDA wagons from Parkandilllack bound for St. Blazey. In the foreground, the main line continues from Burngullow to Probus as single track. (RW 06/98)

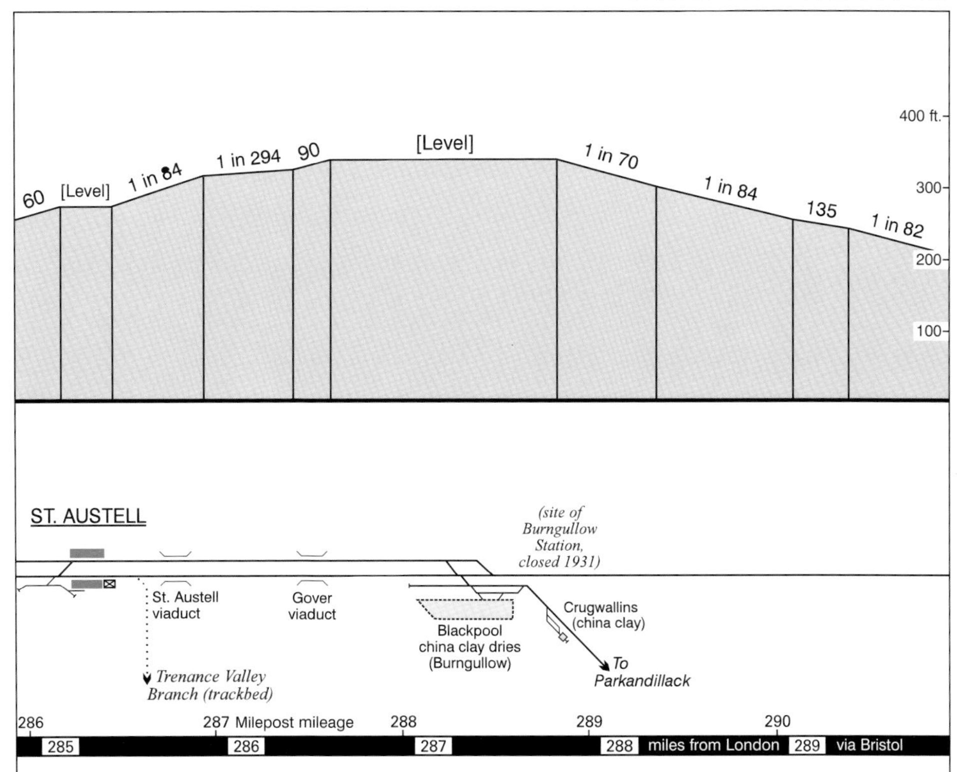

ST. AUSTELL : Motorail trains were once a common sight in Cornwall bringing holiday makers and their cars to a terminal at St. Austell. This was situated on the up side of the station, where now only rusted tracks remain, as 150263 passes on a Penzance to Exeter service. Note the splendid GWR wrought iron footbridge and the white china clay hills visible in the background. (DM 04/99)

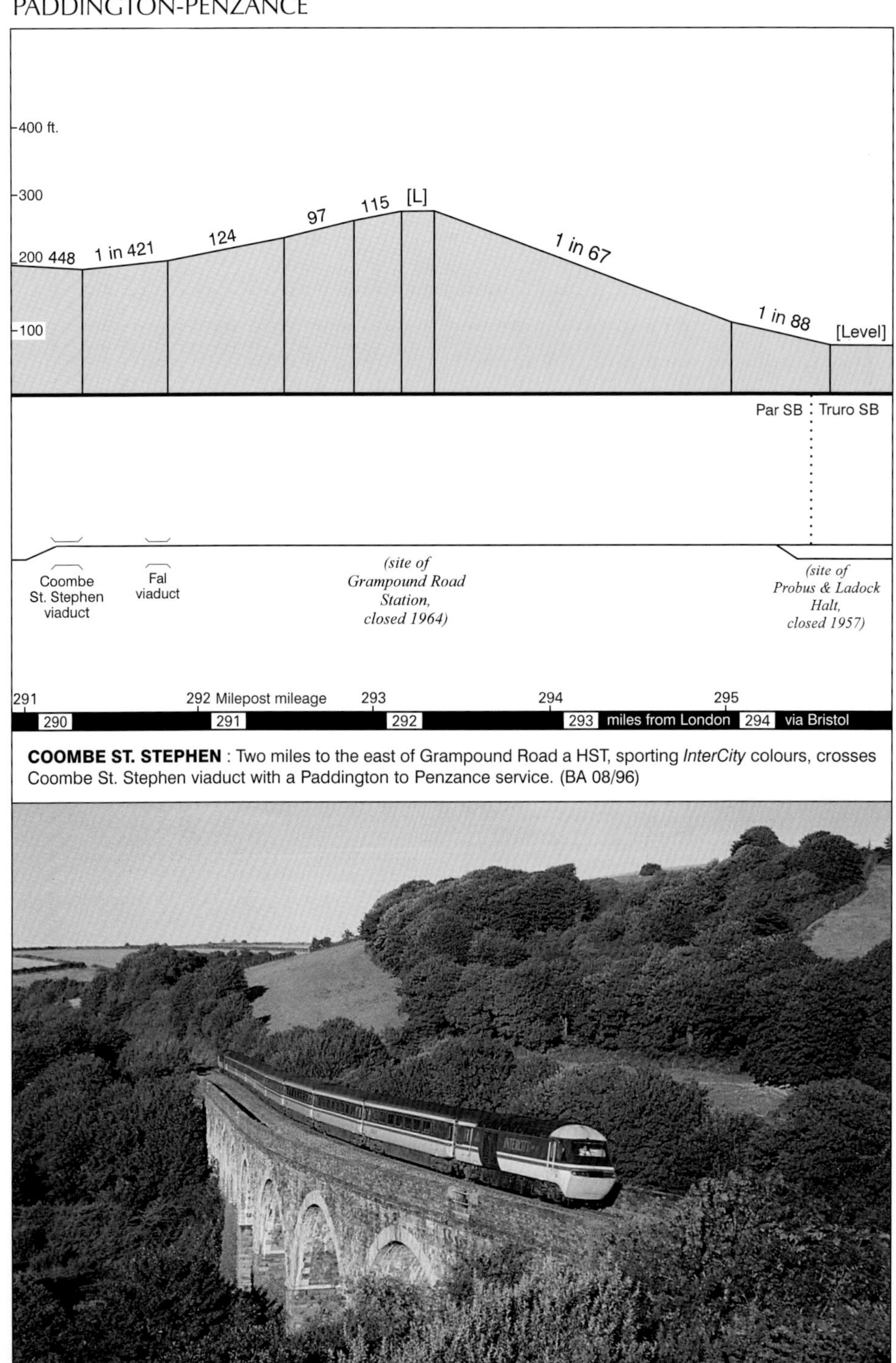

COOMBE ST. STEPHEN : Two miles to the east of Grampound Road a HST, sporting *InterCity* colours, crosses Coombe St. Stephen viaduct with a Paddington to Penzance service. (BA 08/96)

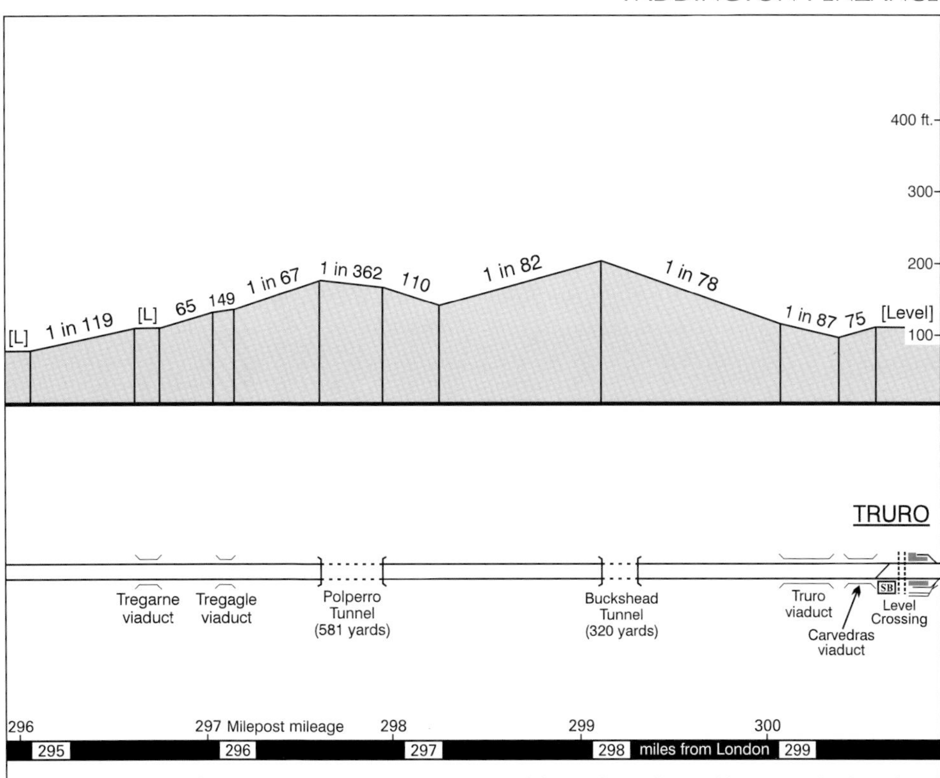

TRURO : The magnificent cathedral at Truro, county town of Cornwall, dominates this panoramic view of an unidentified class 47 heading 1C92, the 1930 Penzance to Bristol TPO. (BA 06/96)

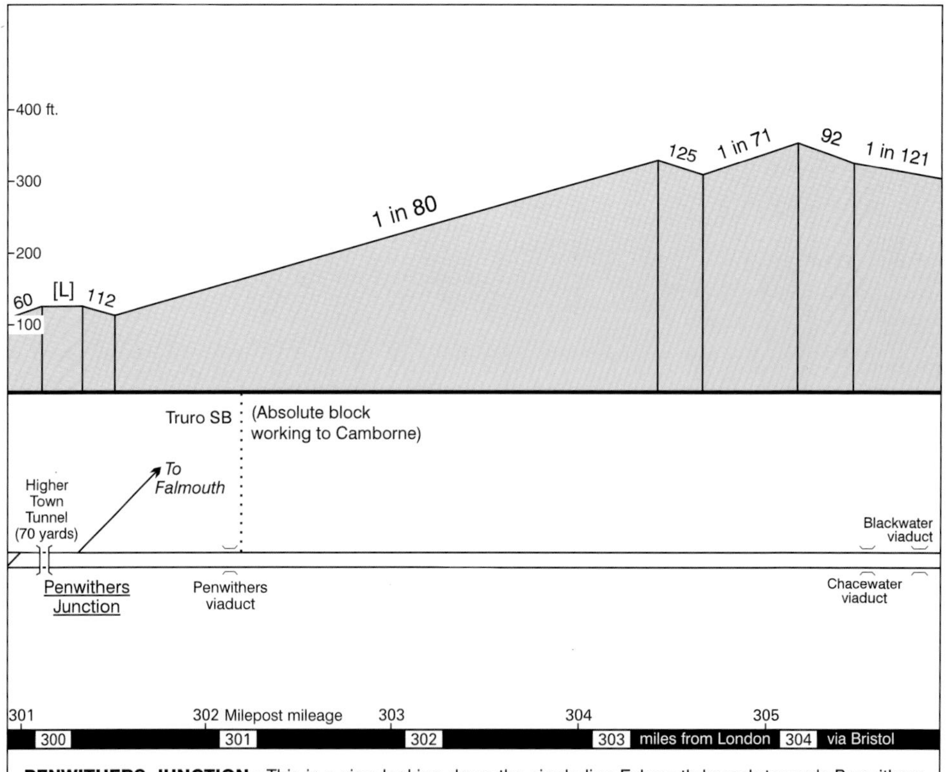

PENWITHERS JUNCTION : This is a view looking down the single line Falmouth branch towards Penwithers Junction and Highertown Tunnel, just over ½ a mile to the west of Truro station. (BA 06/00)

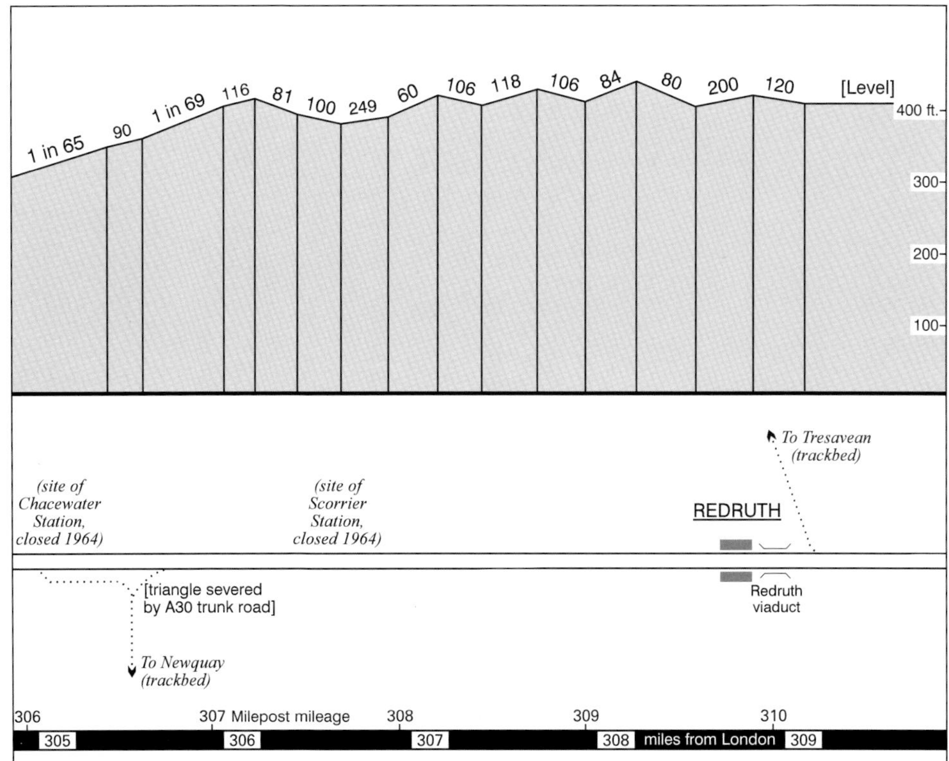

SCORRIER : There are many derelict remains in Cornwall which provide evidence of the Cornish mining industry. One good example is the old engine house at Wheal Busy, Scorrier, where 158871 is seen passing on the way to Penzance with a *Wales & West* service from Cardiff. (BA 08/95)

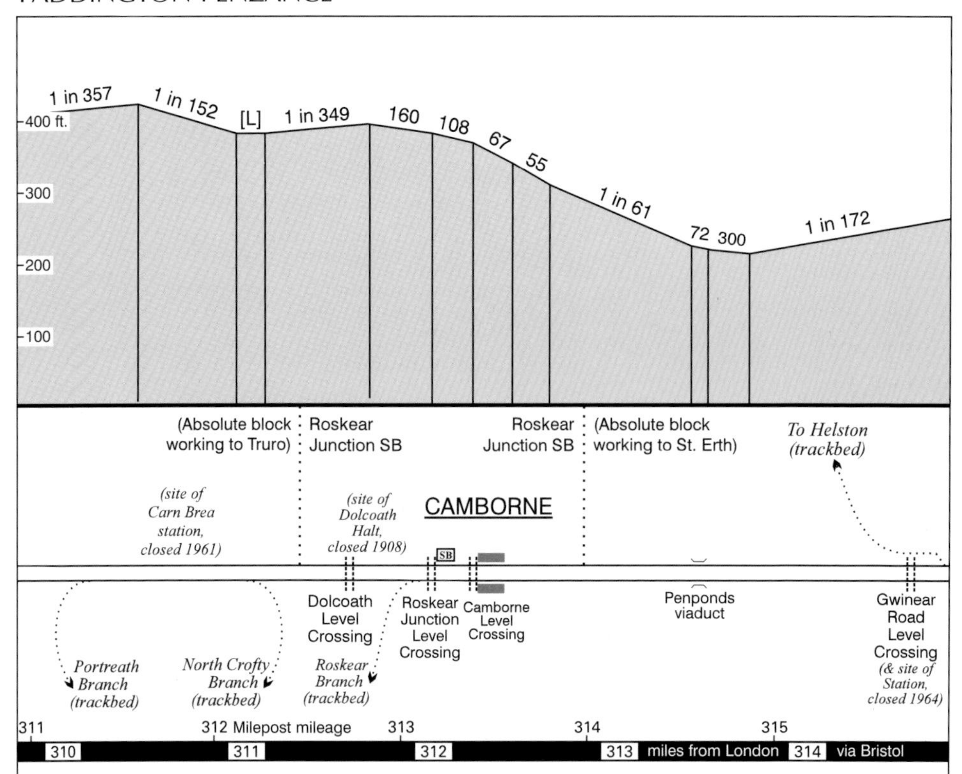

POOL : *Fragonset* liveried 47701 passes Pool, South Crofty, between Redruth and Camborne, with 1V46, the 1017 Manchester to Penzance. South Crofty gained its place in history by having the last operational tin mine in Europe. (BA /98)

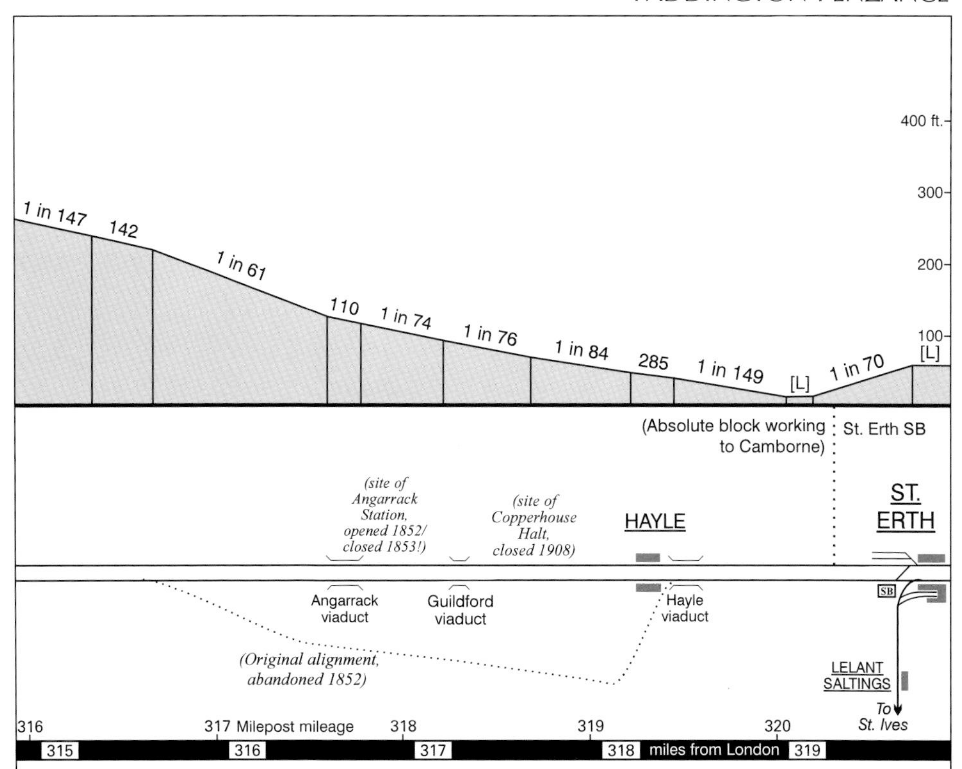

HAYLE : Looking across the small harbour and waste ground (site of the old Hayle foundry), an unidentified class 47 diesel locomotive crosses the magnificent Hayle viaduct with the evening postal from Penzance to Bristol. (BA 05/96)

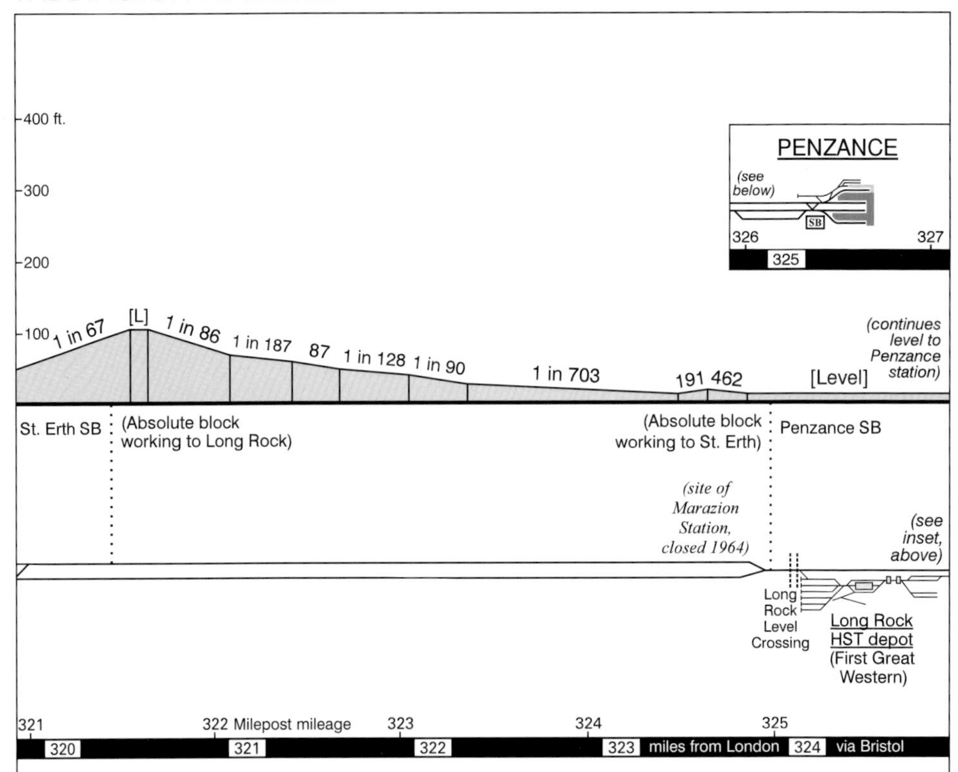

PENZANCE : Journey's end, but the start of one for two class 47 locomotives seen awaiting departure at Penzance station. In the foreground, 47816 *Bristol Bath Road* heads the 'Up Midnight' sleeper service to Paddington, whilst 47626 is in charge of the 'up' Bristol TPO. (BA 06/95)

Gallery

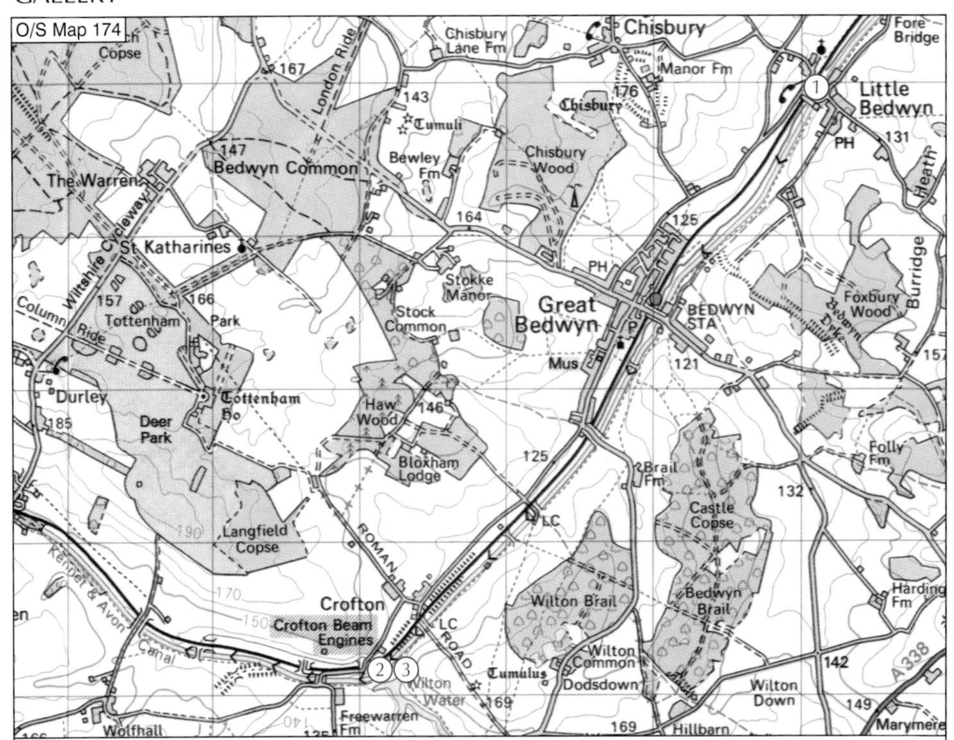

① **LITTLE BEDWYN** : One could argue that this view of Little Bedwyn has an almost 'chocolate box' appearance and is quintessentially English; 59005 *Kenneth J Painter* heads 7C75, the 1248 Acton to Whatley stone empties, beside a partially frozen Kennet & Avon Canal. (MB 01/00)

(2) **CROFTON** : The main line runs near and often parallel to the Kennet & Avon Canal between Southcote Junction and Pewsey. At Crofton, 43190 (above) is seen heading the up "Golden Hind" service on the embankment above the canal, on which there are three narrow boats moored beside the towpath, headed by the colourful 'Leonora' from the Oxford Canal. The building in the picture is Crofton pumping station, home to a working museum with coal-fired beam engines. (MB 06/00)

(3) Looking in the opposite direction, 59102 *Village of Chantry* (below) leans into 'Crofton Curve' in charge of 6V18, the 1239 Hither Green – Whatley stone empties. (MB 01/00)

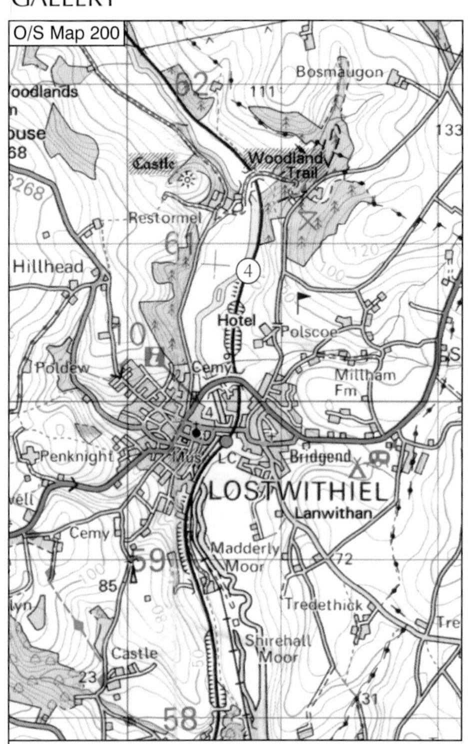

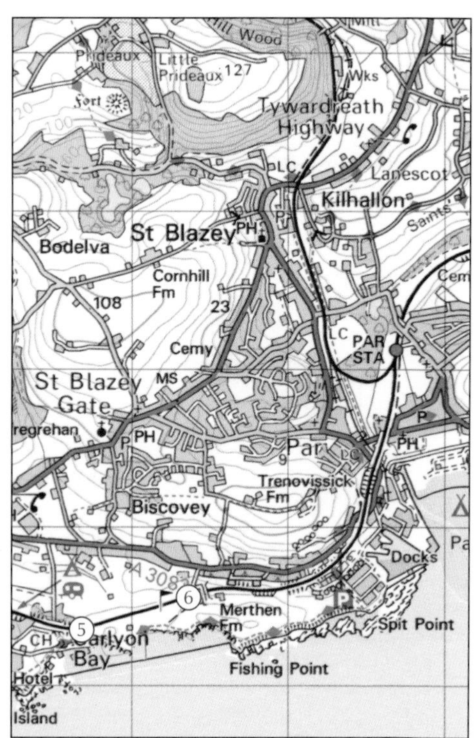

④ **LOSTWITHIEL** : This aerial view shows an *InterCity* liveried HST on a Penzance to Paddington service passing the well mown fairways of Lostwithiel golf course, including a water hazard which no doubt accounts for many lost golf balls from distracted golfers! (BA 06/95)

(5) **CARLYON BAY** : The 'links' golf course at Carlyon Bay, on the coast between Par and St. Austell, affords excellent photographic opportunities. A panoramic view shows 66106 (above) on a Drinnick to Fowey trip working, with St. Austell visible in the background and, in particular, the large white building of English China Clay's headquarters. (BA 12/99)

(6) Heading westwards, 37671 *Tre Pol and Pen* (below) hauls a rake of CDA wagons from Fowey back to Treviscoe. (RW 01/98)

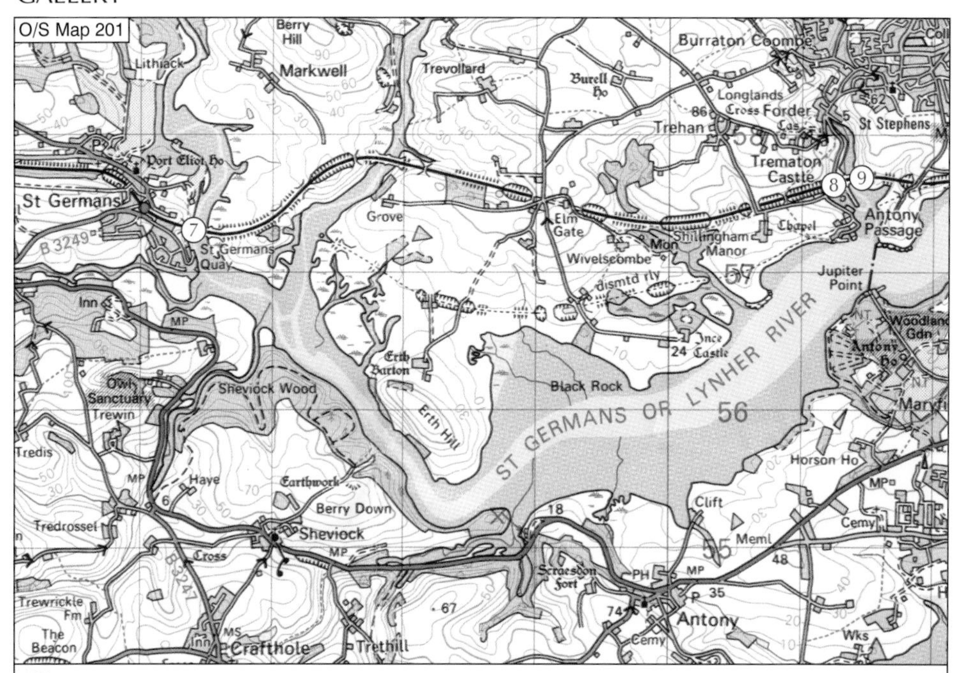

ⓐ **ST. GERMANS VIADUCT** : Viaducts abound in Cornwall. Looking across the river mouth towards St. Germans Quay, a Penzance to Paddington HST crosses St. Germans viaduct, beneath which the River Tiddy flows into the St. Germans River, or Lynher as it is also known. (RW 07/97)

(8) **FORDER VIADUCT** : Built in 1908, Forder viaduct makes a splendid composition from the north side of the main line as 66123 (above) heads over the viaduct with 6C21, the1417 Newport ADJ to St. Blazey 'Enterprise' service. A massive dockyard crane at Devonport dominates the skyline. (BA 07/99)

(9) Photographed with Trematon Castle on the hillside in the background, 60053 *Nordic Terminal* (below) crosses the viaduct at the head of 6B68, the 0940 Burngullow to Newport ADJ china clay tanks, which will eventually go on to Irvine in Ayrshire. (BA 11/99)

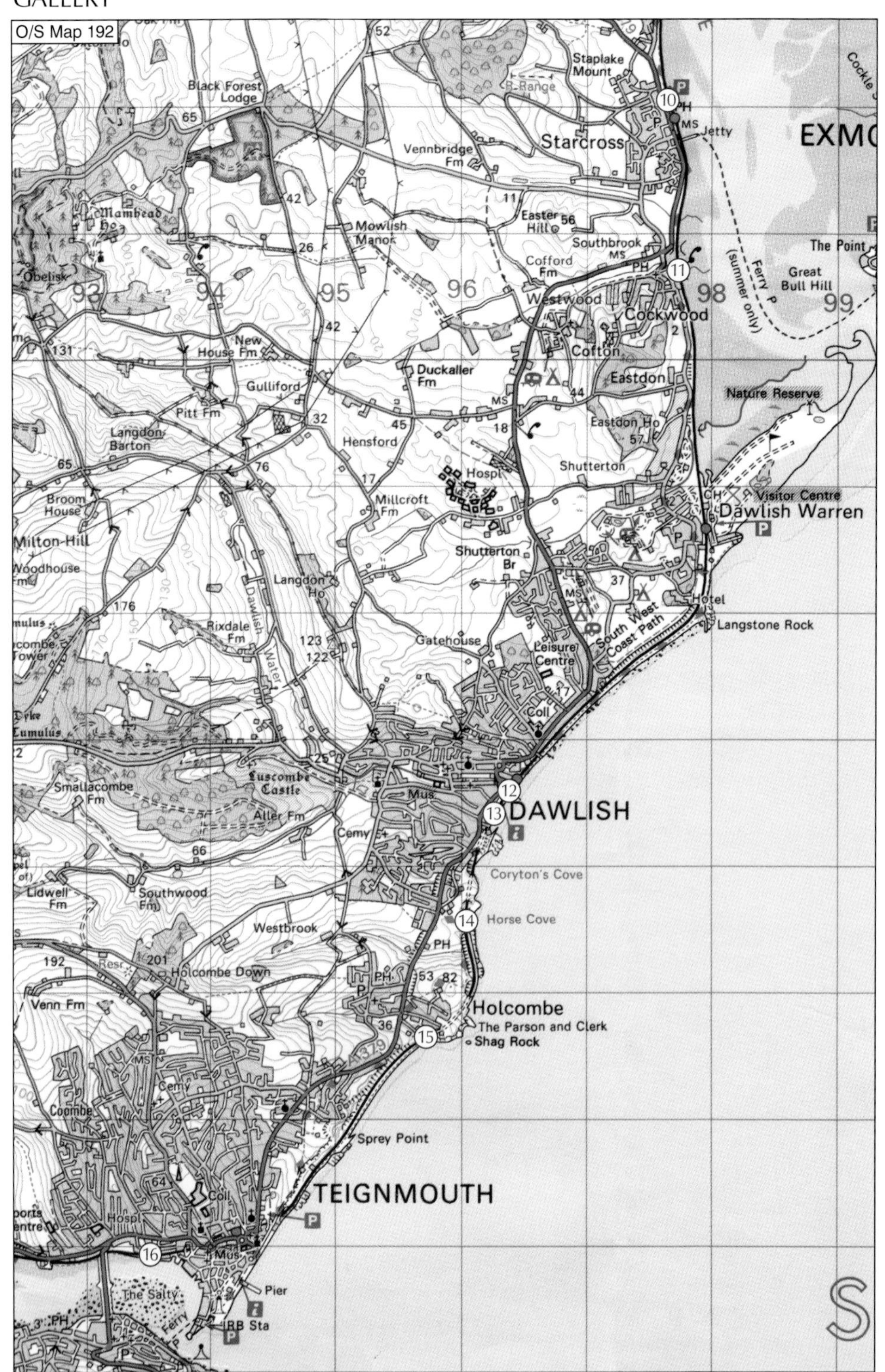
O/S Map 192
Black Forest Lodge
Staplake Mount
Starcross
Jetty
EXMO
Vennbridge Fm
Mamhead Ho
Obelisk
Mowlish Manor
Easter Hill
Southbrook
Cofford Fm
The Point
Ferry (summer only)
Great Bull Hill
Westwood
Cockwood
Cofton
New House Fm
Duckaller Fm
Eastdon
Nature Reserve
Gulliford
Pitt Fm
Langdon Barton
Hensford
Eastdon Ho
Shutterton
Hospl
Broom House
Millcroft Fm
Visitor Centre
Dawlish Warren
Milton Hill
Woodhouse Fm
Shutterton Br
Langdon Ho
Dawlish Water
Rixdale Fm
Gatehouse
Leisure Centre
South West Coast Path
Hotel
Langstone Rock
Luscombe Castle
Smallacombe Fm
Aller Fm
Mus
Cemy
DAWLISH
Coryton's Cove
Lidwell Fm
Southwood Fm
Westbrook
Horse Cove
Holcombe Down
Venn Fm
Holcombe
The Parson and Clerk
Shag Rock
Coombe
Sprey Point
TEIGNMOUTH
Hospl
Coll
The Salty
Ferry
Pier
IRB Sta

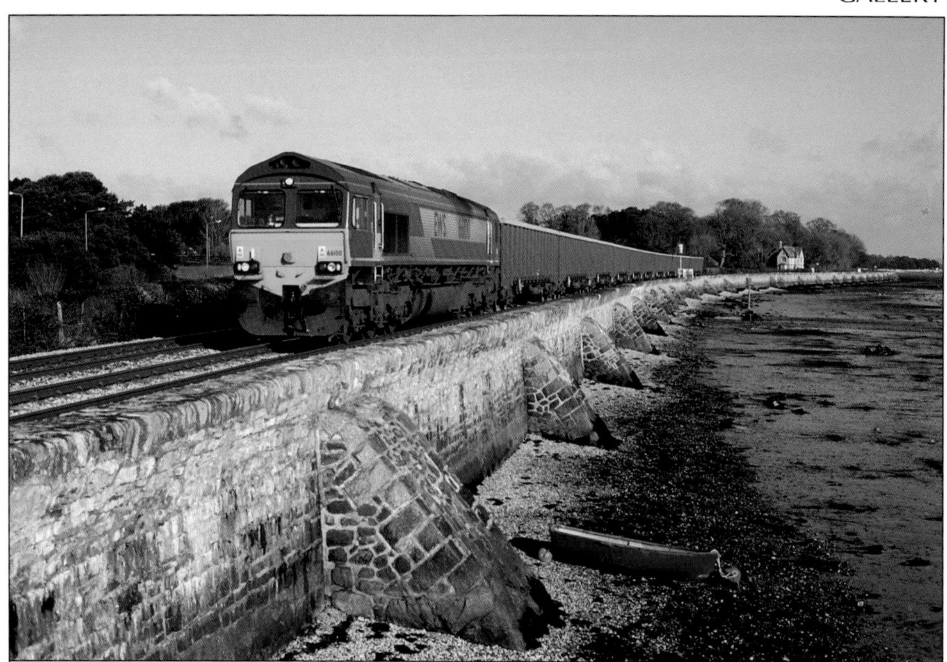

⑩ **STARCROSS** : This location provides the first opportunity to photograph trains alongside the sea wall before the well-known stretch between Dawlish and Teignmouth. Approaching Starcross, 66100 heads for Newton Abbot with a special stone working (7Z94) from Westbury to Hackney Yard. (DM 03/00)

⑪ **COCKWOOD HARBOUR** : An embankment, separating Cockwood harbour and the Exe estuary, carries the West of England main line at Cockwood, and is one of the most photographed locations in the country. 67014 was photographed here heading 1E43, the 1509 Plymouth to Low Fell mail. (DM 08/00)

⑫ **DAWLISH** : Looking back towards Dawlish station and the sandstone outcrop of Langstone Rock in the far distance, this view depicts 60096 *Ben Macdui* returning empty china clay polybulks from Exeter Riverside to St. Blazey. (RW 06/96)

(13) **DAWLISH** : This elevated view, photographed from a footpath high above the bay on the opposite side of the railway line, shows 47830 passing through Dawlish on a glorious summer's day with 1C19, the 0933 Paddington to Penzance Motorail. (DM 08/00)

(14) **CLERK'S TUNNEL** : Sporting black diamond coal sector decals, 37696 emerges from the west portal of Clerk's Tunnel with 6V70, the 0850 Bescot to St. Blazey china clay empties. This classic location is also commonly referred to as Horse Cove. (RW 05/95)

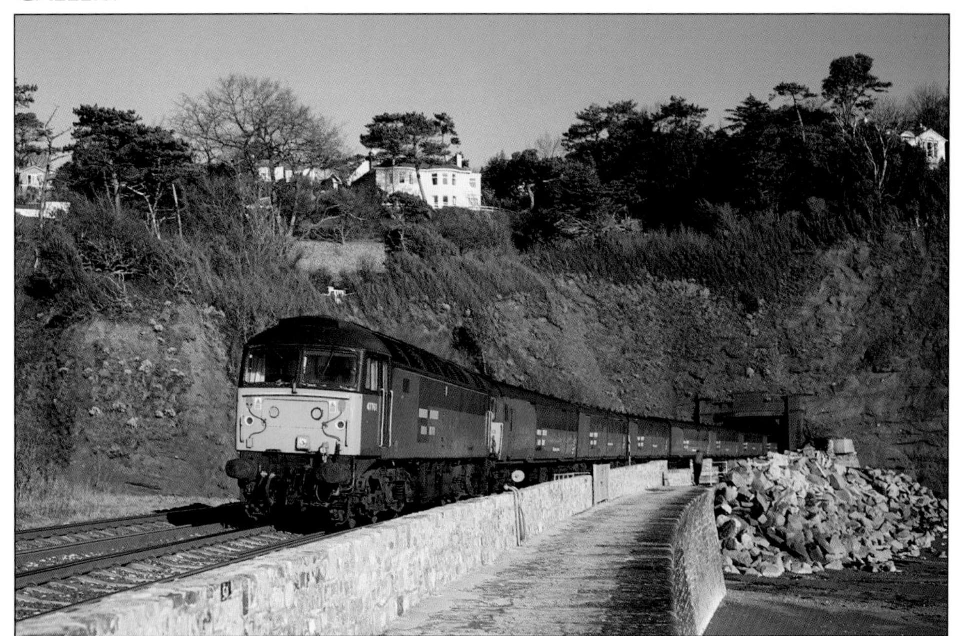

⑮ **HOLCOMBE** : In Summer 2000, all mail services were recast following the introduction of class 67s and the opening of a new Royal Mail Terminal at Bristol Parkway. Sadly, this spelt the end of 5C99, the 1220 Bristol to Plymouth empty mail vans, a popular train service amongst rail photographers, seen here leaving Parson's Tunnel at Holcombe with 47761 at the head. (RW 01/99)

⑯ **TEIGNMOUTH** : The final 'Gallery' photograph is a view taken from the A379 Shaldon road bridge, which crosses the River Teign. Headed by 43179 *Pride of Laira*, a HST leaves Teignmouth along the north bank of the river with 1C17, the 0845 Paddington to Penzance. (DM 08/00)

Berks & Hants

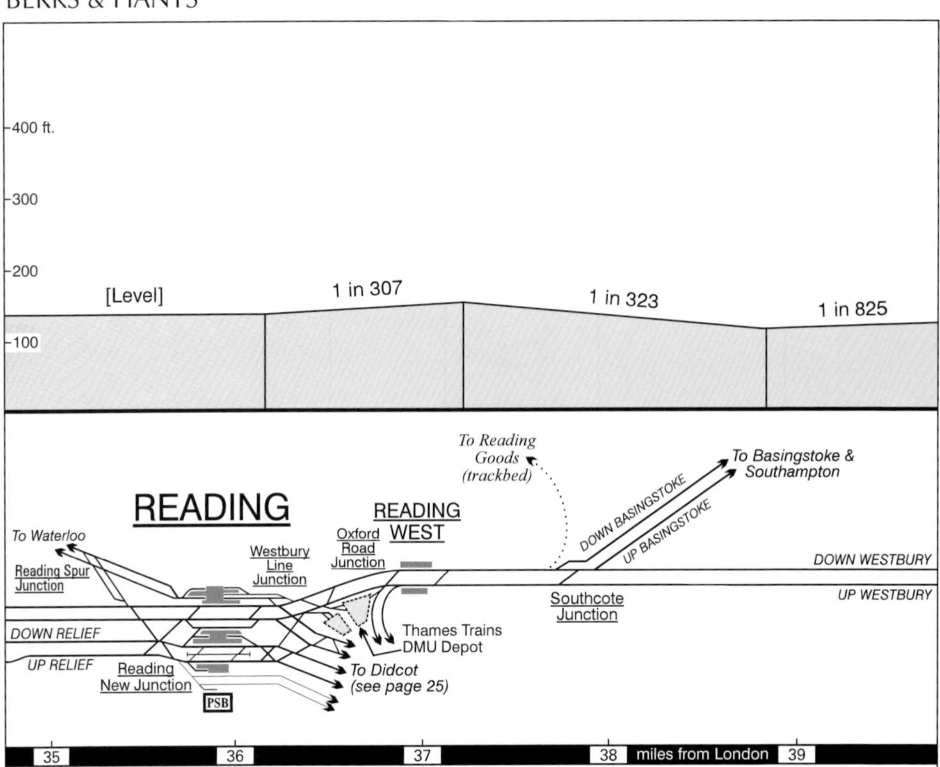

READING WEST : This view, looking north from the overbridge at Reading West station, shows the layout at Oxford Road Junction behind which 166206 is stabled at Reading Depot. (MB 03/00)

SOUTHCOTE JUNCTION : The 2-mile section between Reading and Southcote Junction is a busy stretch of track, handling cross-country services running to and from the South Coast as well as traffic bound for the 'Berks & Hants'. At the junction itself, 159015 (above) meets 47828 heading the southbound "Pines Express"; a passenger service which does not call at Reading General, running direct between Reading West Junction and Reading West. (MB 04/00)

Prior to a repaint into *Mendip Rail* green and orange livery, 59002 *Alan J Day* (below) is seen in close up at the junction with 7V67, the 1033 Sevington to Westbury stone empties. (MB 04/00)

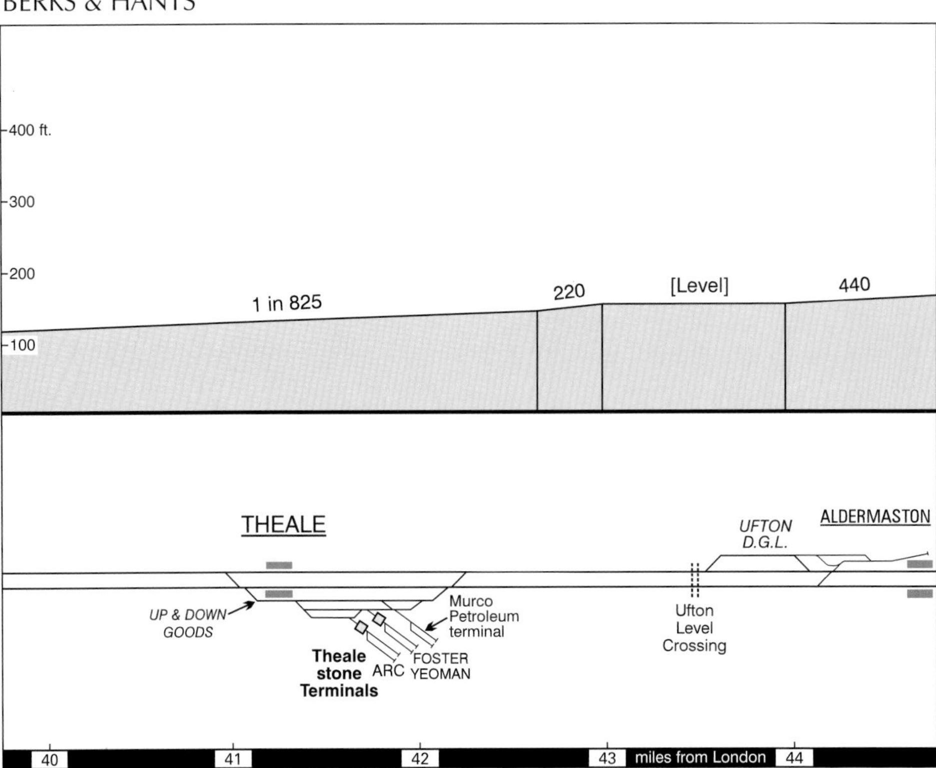

THEALE : Although the main line is cast in shadow, the early morning sun shines brightly on the up & down goods loop directly beside the signal gantry and the sidings which give access to the oil and stone terminals. A run-round must first be undertaken before 59101 *Village of Whatley* can leave Theale with 7C31, the 0913 stone empties bound for Merehead. (MB 04/00)

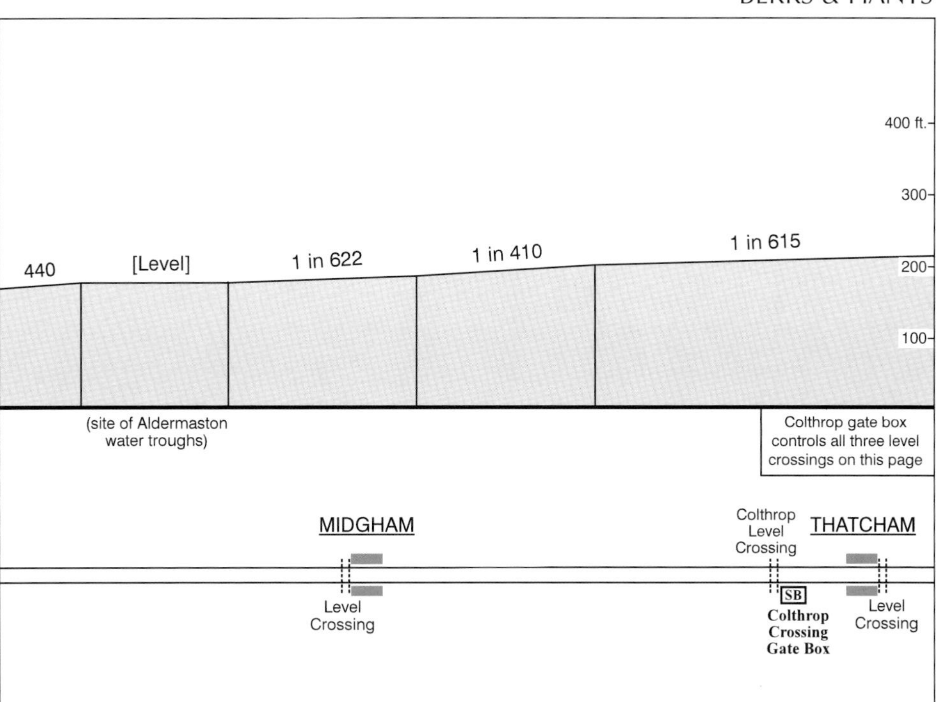

COLTHROP : The signal box is still operational at Colthrop, which also controls the crossings at Midgham and Thatcham. A paper mill dominates the background as 59005 *Kenneth J Painter* approaches Colthrop crossing whilst working 7A09, the 0705 Merehead to Acton. (MB 04/00)

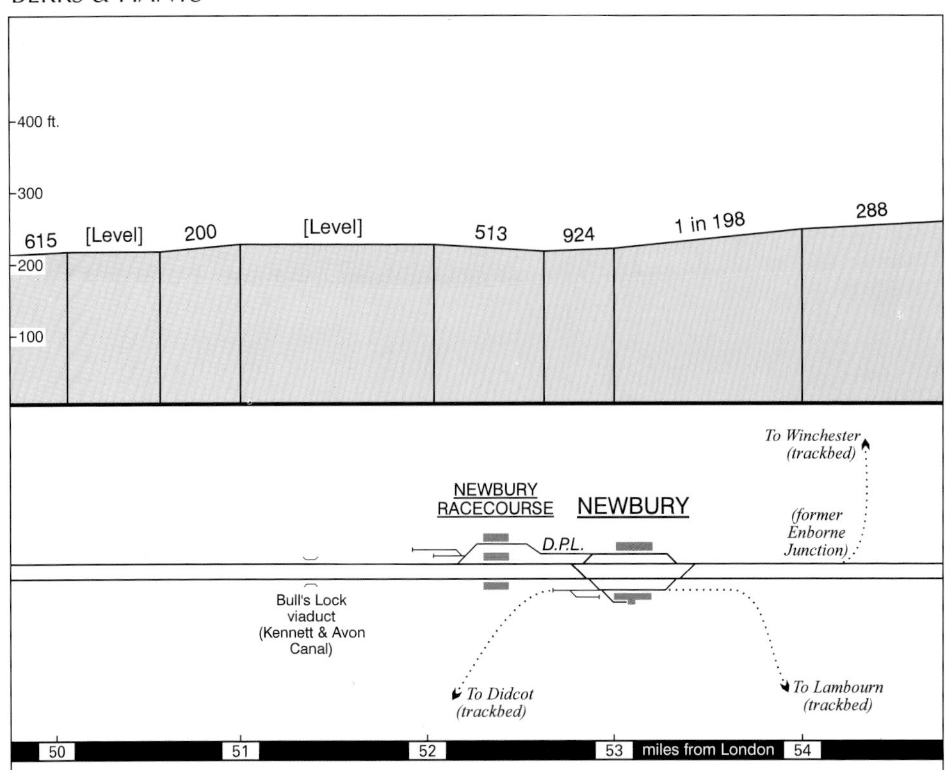

NEWBURY RACECOURSE : The Berkshire town of Newbury has two stations and it is Newbury Racecourse which gives punters direct access from the train to the course; any race-day charter train being "stabled" in the 'down' passenger loop. In this view, 47772 + 47778 *Irresistible* 'top-n-tail' the *Serco* test train through Newbury Racecourse. (MB 06/00)

NEWBURY : Unique to the 'Berks & Hants', the up and down fast lines run between the main platform lines at Newbury station, where 59001 *Yeoman Endeavour* (above) is seen approaching with 7A17, the 1055 Merehead to Acton. Note the bell on the front of the Class 59, reminiscent of one carried by two famous steam locomotives, 6000 *King George V* and 60010 *Dominion of Canada*. (MB 06/00)

Looking in the opposite direction, 47815 (below) leaves Newbury station in charge of 1C44, the 1403 Paddington to Plymouth and passes 59102 *Village of Chantry* waiting to proceed with 7V67, the 1033 Sevington to Merehead stone empties. (MB 06/00)

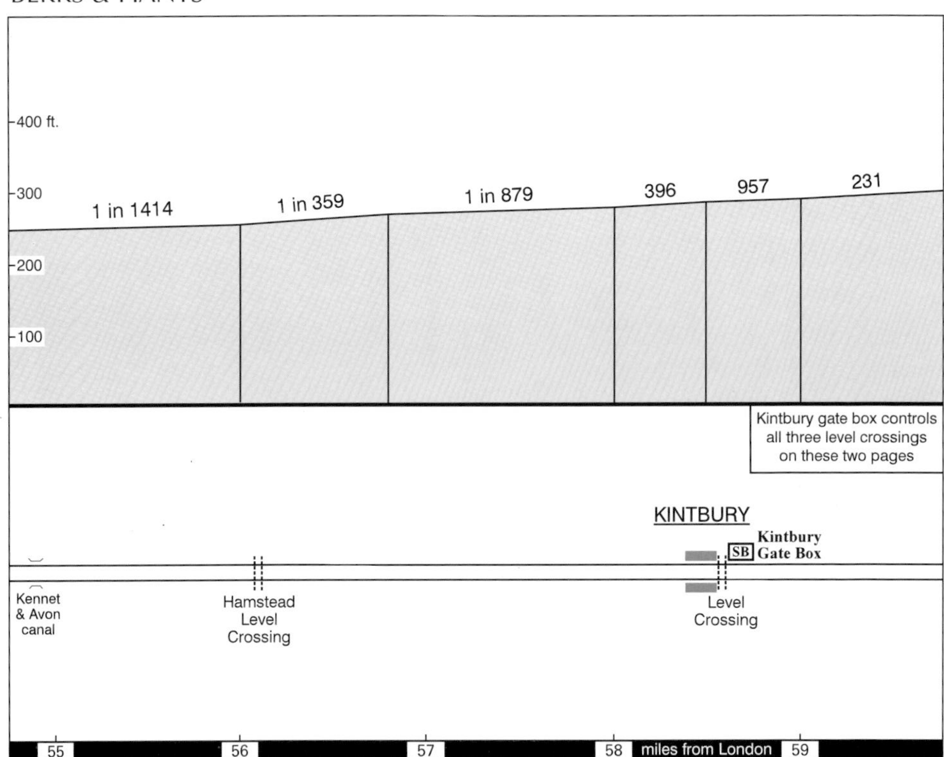

KINTBURY : Road access to Kintbury from the A4 is by means of a level crossing immediately to the west of Kintbury station. The barriers are operated from a small cabin, partially visible to the right of the crossing, which 1A54, the 1230 Plymouth to Paddington HST service is about to pass. Like Colthrop, Kintbury box also controls two other crossings - Hamstead and Hungerford. (MB 03/00)

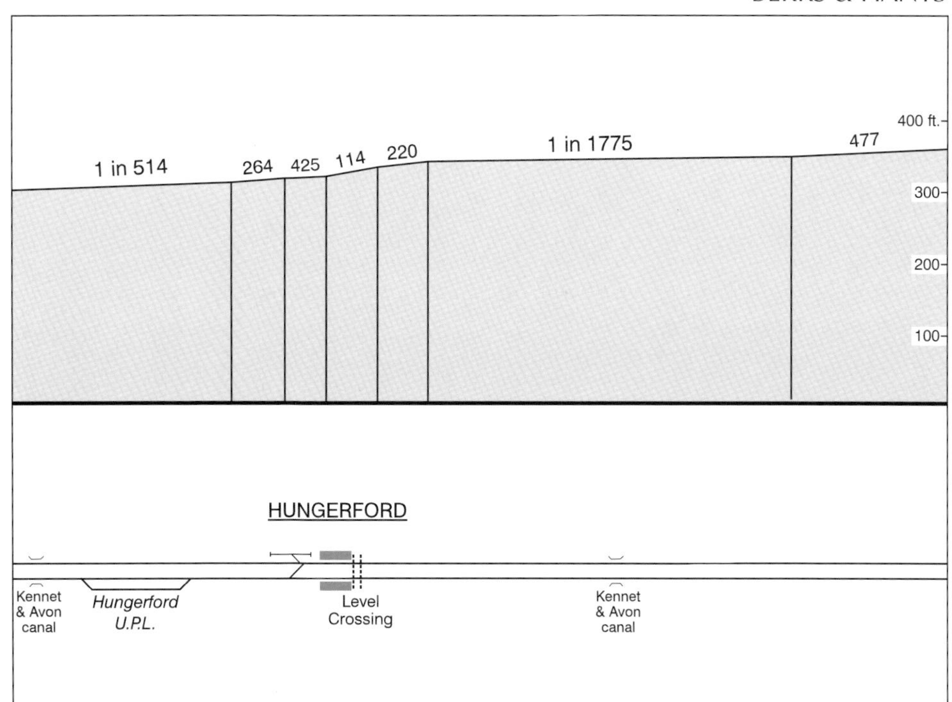

HUNGERFORD : *Thames Trains* run frequent day-time services which call at the intermediate stations between Bedwyn and Reading. A 3-car Network Express Turbo unit, No.165107, slows to pick up passengers at Hungerford with one of these services. Note the burnt out passenger shelter. (MB 02/00)

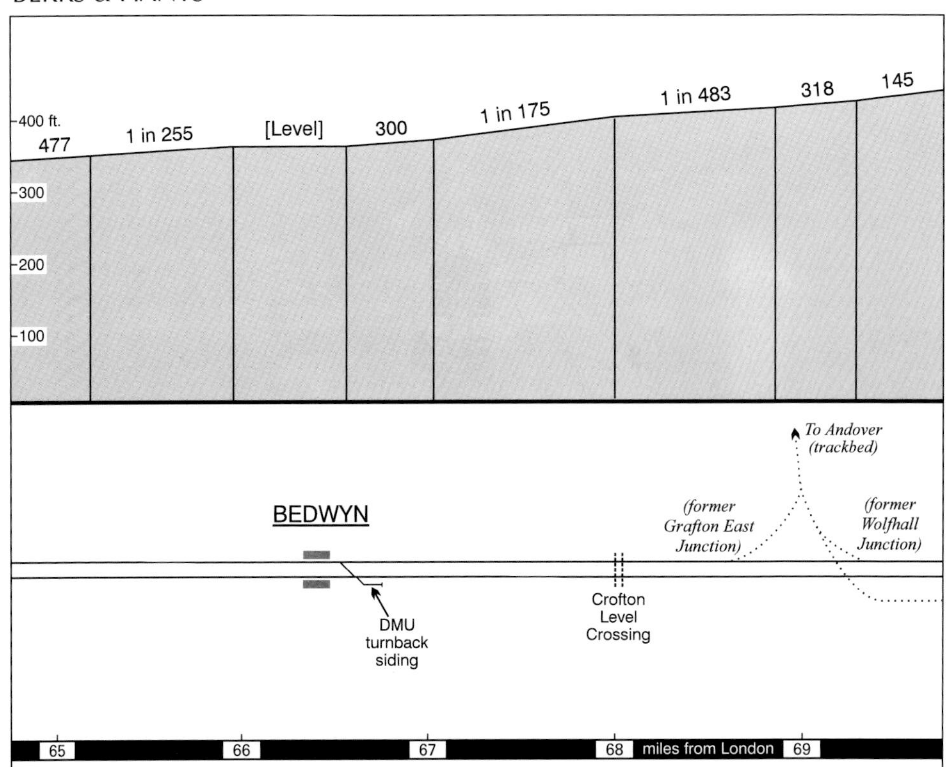

BEDWYN : With the church spire at Little Bedwyn visible in the background, 59004 *Paul A Hammond* passes through (Great) Bedwyn with 7C75, the 1248 Acton Yard to Whatley stone empties, made up of box wagons and 'Jumbo' hoppers. On the down side of the main line you can see the Kennet & Avon Canal, which is at a higher level than the railway. (MB 06/00)

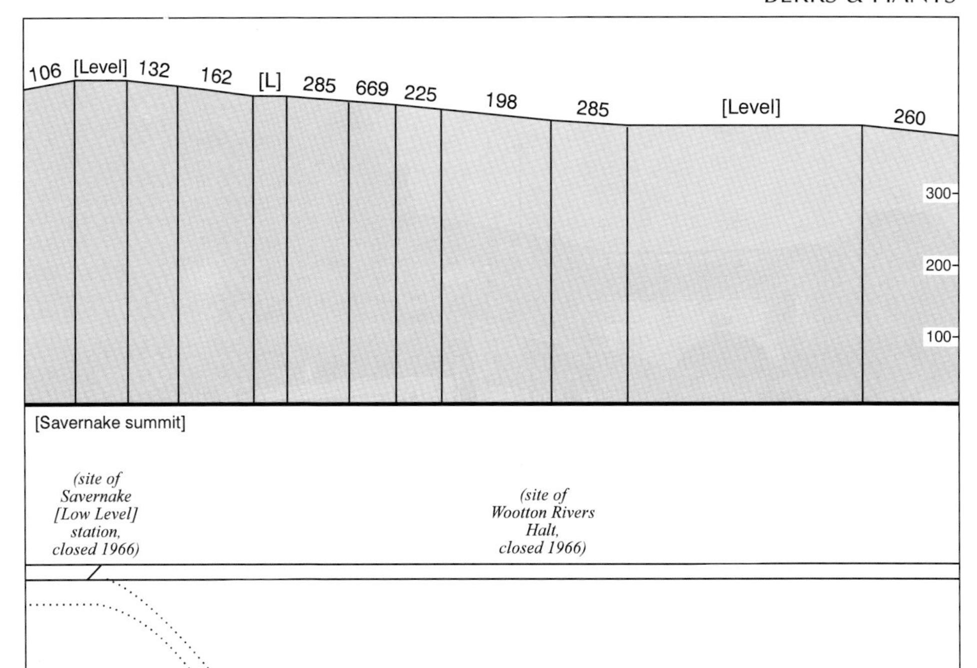

SAVERNAKE : The highest point the 'Berks & Hants' reaches above sea level is at Savernake, where 59004 *Paul A Hammond* is seen again, but this time in charge of 7A17, the 1055 Merehead to Acton yard loaded bogie hoppers. The train is approaching the site of Savernake Low level station, where the trackbed of the line to Marlborough once trailed in to the right of the picture. (MB 02/00)

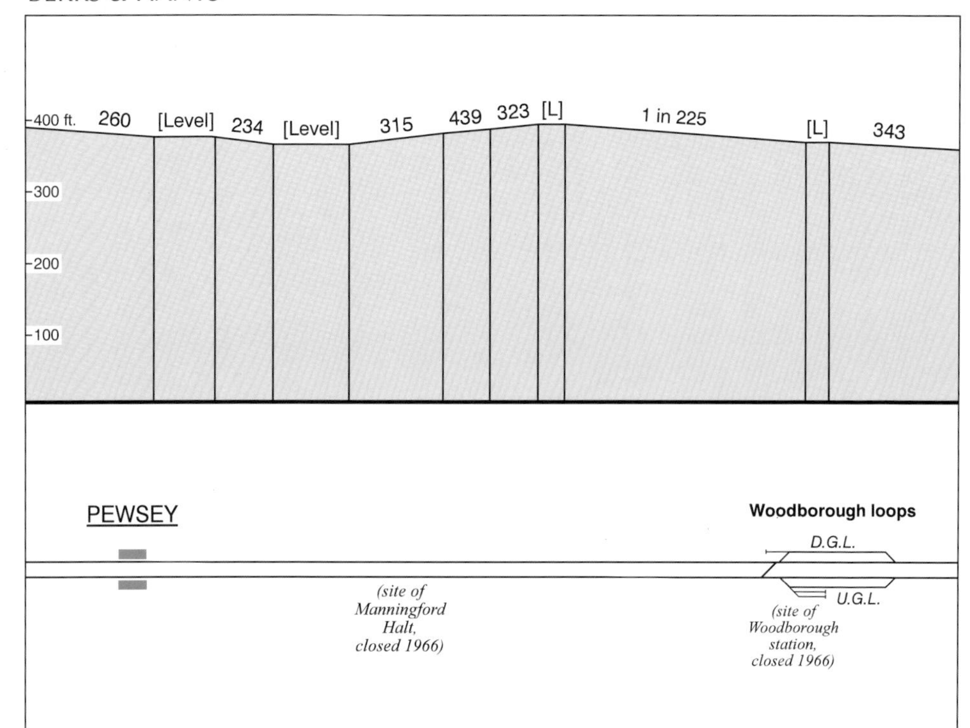

PEWSEY : An unidentified HST enters Pewsey station at speed with the up "Golden Hind", 1A27, the 0515 Penzance to Paddington. This particular stretch of line through the Vale of Pewsey has always been associated with fast running and it is not uncommon for diesel hauled passenger trains to exceed the magic 'ton'! (MB 03/00)

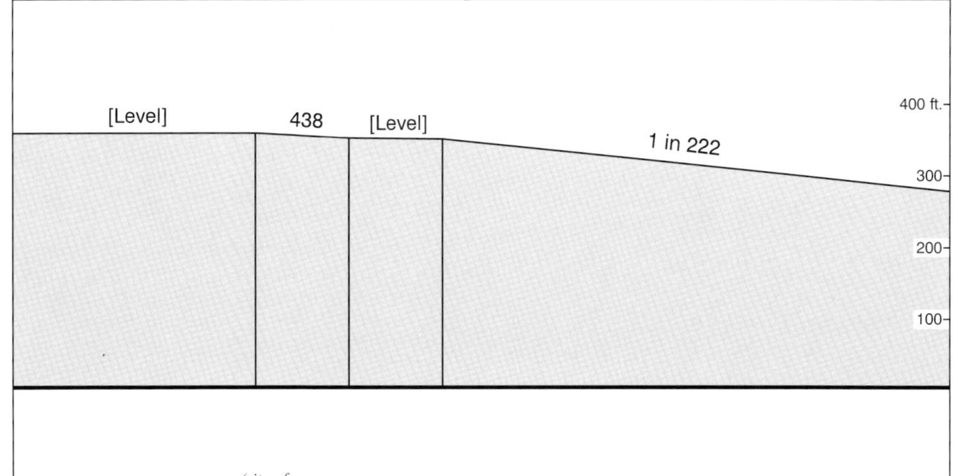

WOODBOROUGH : A train of loaded hoppers hauled by 59001 *Yeoman Endeavour* has been stopped in the Up Goods Loop at Woodborough to allow the approaching 1A46, 0820 Penzance – Paddington service to overtake. A plan of Woodborough Loops is shown on the opposite page. (MB 02/00)

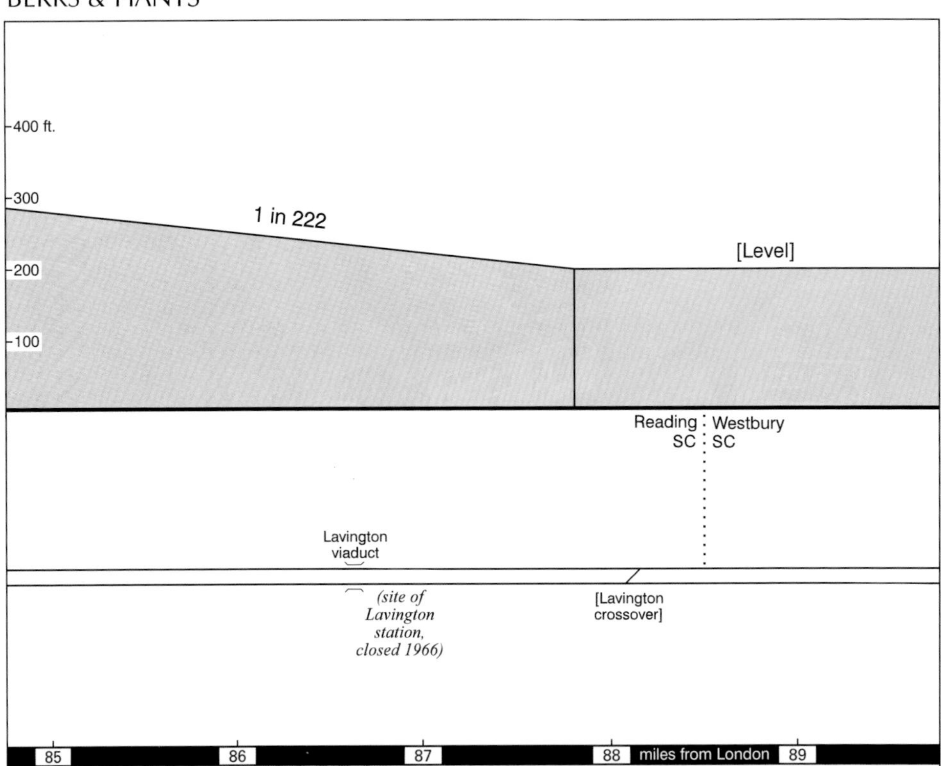

LAVINGTON : Driver training for handling vacuum braked trains resulted in 31203 unusually working on the 'Berks & Hants' with a rake of ZKV tipplers originating from West Drayton. The train is seen at Lavington and the industrial unit in the background marks the site of the old station. (SM 03/99)

400 ft.
300
[Level] 1 in 500 [Level] 200
100

(site of Edington & Bratton station, closed 1952)

Heywood Road Junction

Westbury cement works (Blue Circle)

90 91 92 93 miles from London 94

EDINGTON & BRATTON : Sporting contrasting liveries, 37057 *Viking* + 37114 *City of Worcester* pass the site of Edington & Bratton station with 6Z65, the 0820 Merehead to Acton stone train. Note the cement works chimney in the distance – a well-known Westbury landmark. (SM 10/94)

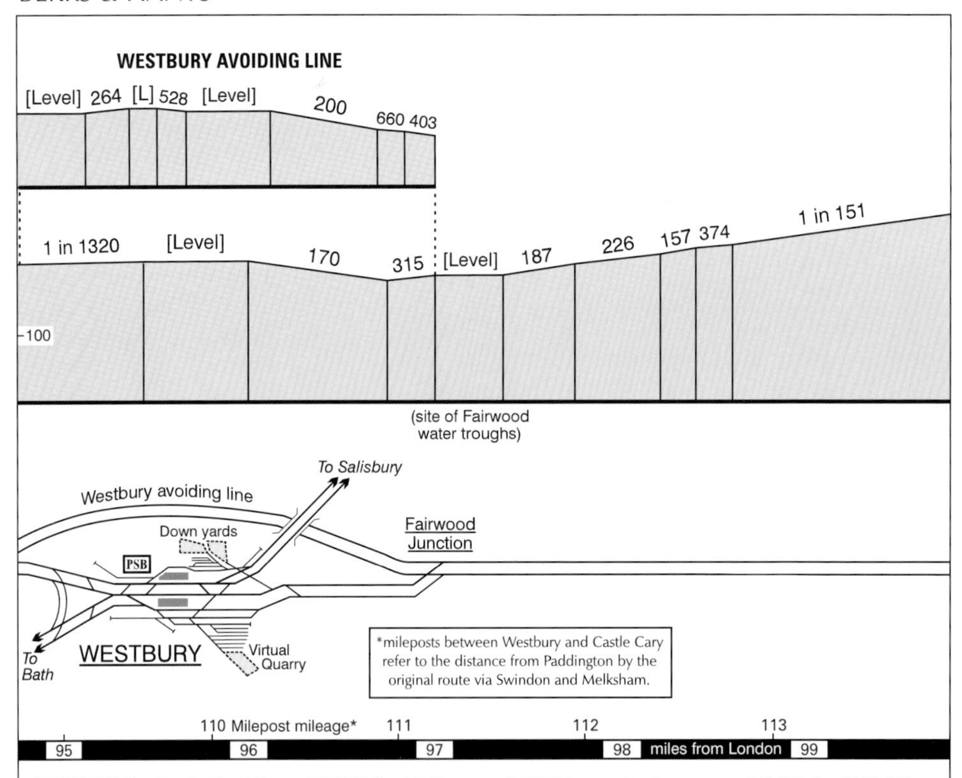

WESTBURY : Due to the failure of 59004 *Paul A Hammond*, 56117 came to the rescue of 6V18, the 1239 Hither Green to Whatley, which is seen hauling the train round the curve from Heywood Road Junction into Westbury; the scene dominated by Westbury panel signalbox. (SM 07/98)

WESTBURY : A panoramic view of the east end of Westbury station sees 150240 (above) leaving with the 0653 Weymouth to Bristol *Wales & West* service, whilst 43137 waits yet further time with the late running 1A22, 0555 Plymouth to Paddington. A total of four class 66 locomotives can also be seen, with 66085+66115 stabled to the right of the station. (MB 04/00)

On the last day of 'booked' class 47 operation, 47217+47338 (below) head 6O92, the 1035 Exeter Riverside to Dollands Moor china clay 'polybulks' on the Westbury avoiding line, which runs between Heywood Road Junction and Fairwood Junction. A pair of class 37s (37250+37692 *The Lass O' Ballochmyle*) can be seen on the 'station' line with a train of stone empties. (SM 11/97)

CLINK ROAD JUNCTION : The single line spur to Frome leaves the main line at Clink Road Junction and is partially visible towards the rear of this picture. At the location, 58011 *Worksop Depot* heads for Westbury and a reversal before retracing this part of the route with 7Z87, the 0745 Merehead to Exeter Riverside loaded bogie boxes. (SM 07/98)

FROME NORTH : The Frome 'Loop' is ostensibly single track, except for the section which gives access to the freight only line to Whatley Quarry, where 47721 St. Bede is seen in charge of 1A37, the 0949 Frome to Paddington *Royal Scotsman*; a luxury charter train that visited Frome and Cranmore (for the West Somerset Railway) on a regular basis. (SM 08/95)

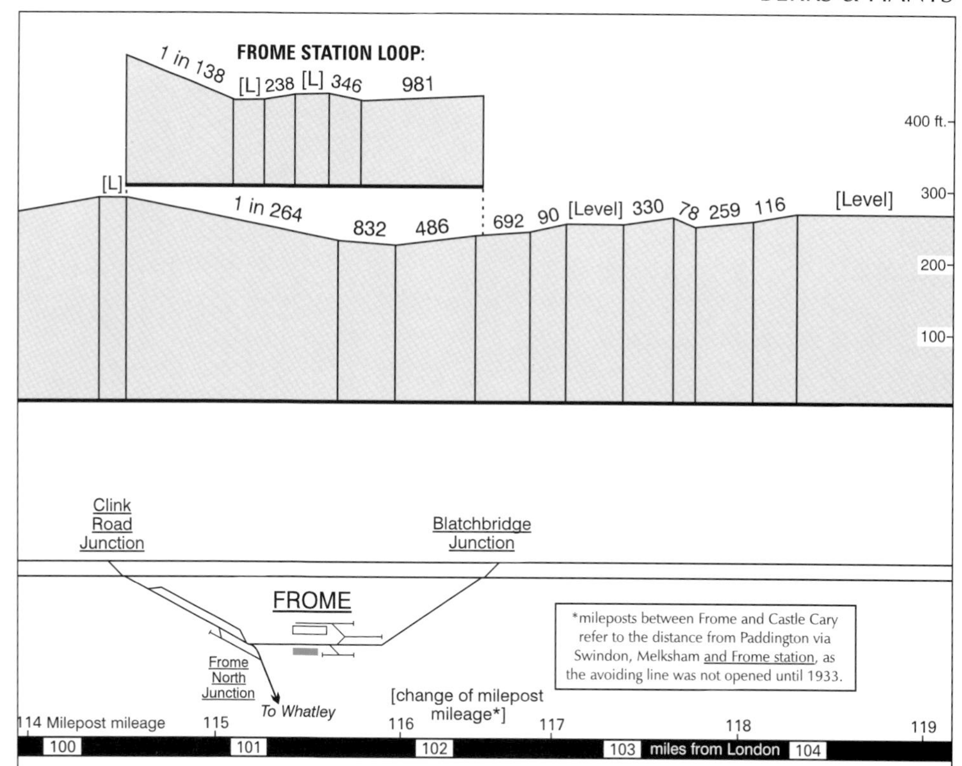

FROME : Frome station has retained its all-over roof and is a splendid historical record of GWR architecture dating back to the 'Broad Gauge' era. In this view, 37114 *City of Worcester* is substituting for the 'booked' Class 37/4, seen at the station with 2O93, the 1633 Bristol to Weymouth. (SM 05/95)

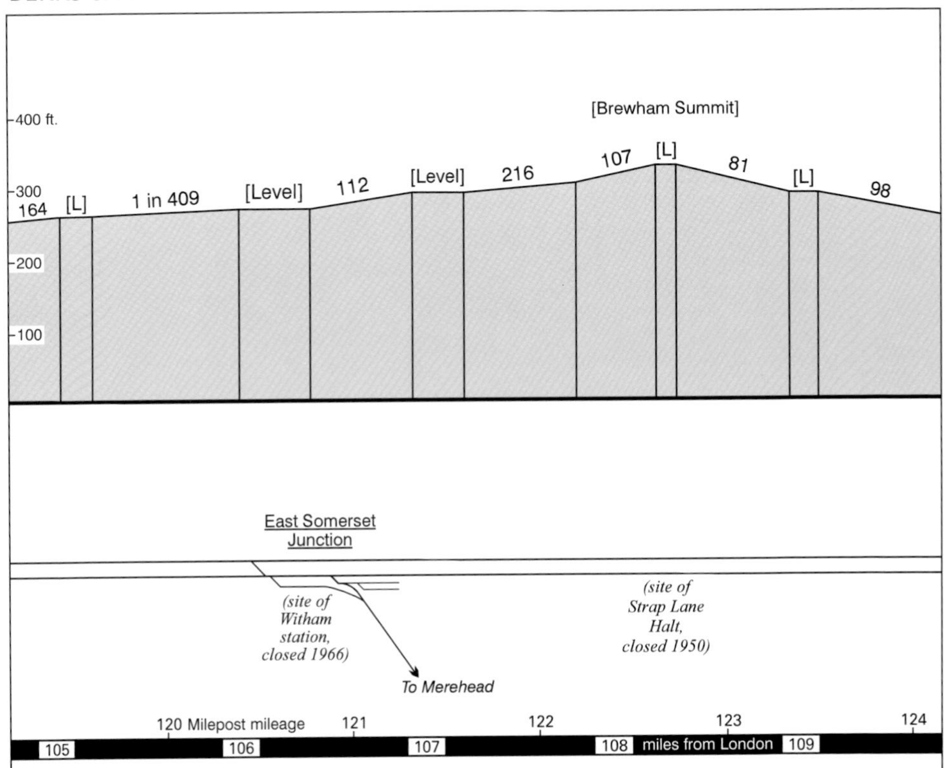

BREWHAM : The second highest point on the 'Berks & Hants' is Brewham Summit. Amidst open countryside, 37431 breasts the summit at the site of Strap Lane Halt with 8C25, the 1315 Merehead to Minehead, conveying boulders for sea defence work at the Somerset resort. (SM 06/96)

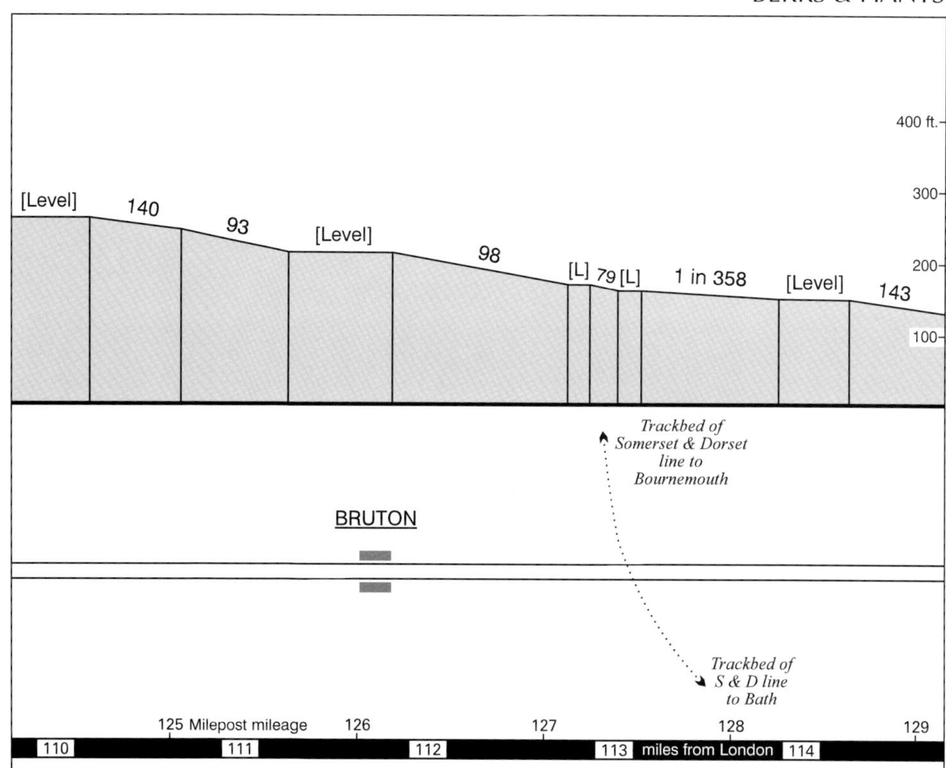

BRUTON : A small number of passengers wait at Bruton for 150254/221 to arrive with the 0839 Weymouth to Bristol Temple Meads service. How many of them will have noticed that the graffiti artist's spelling on the platform overbridge is incorrect! (MB 04/00)

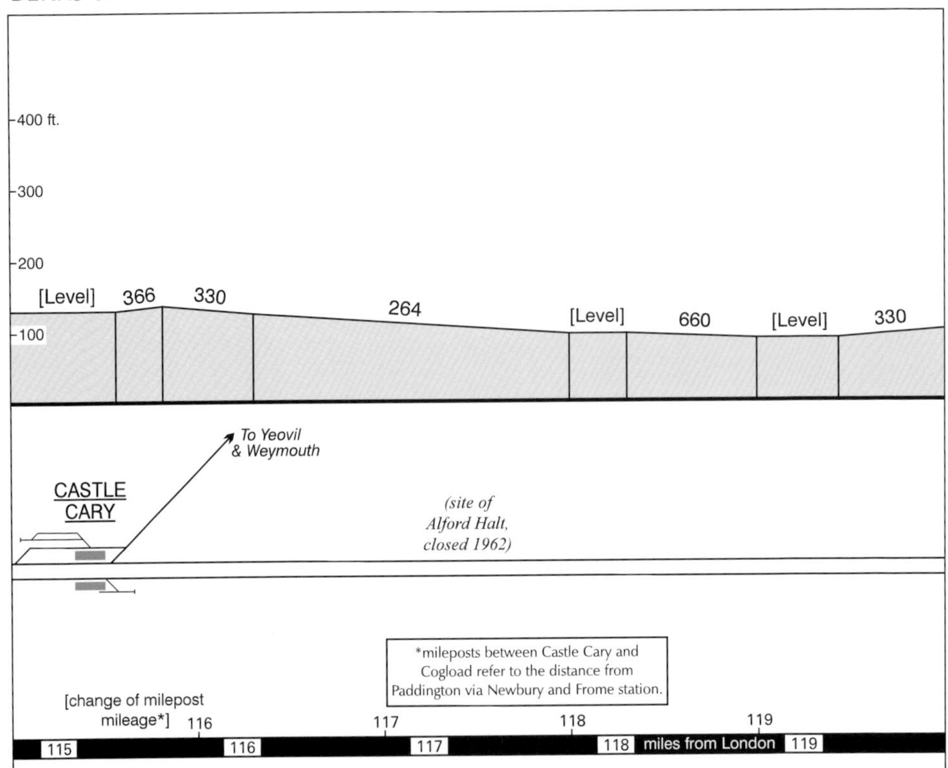

CASTLE CARY : The station at Castle Cary provides a delightful setting for this view of 47846 *THOR* on 1C35, the 1203 Paddington to Penzance Motorail service. The train is passing the junction where the singled branch line to Weymouth leaves the main line. Of note are the two mileposts; MP115½ represents the 'Berks & Hants' mileage from Paddington, whilst MP129¾ is the mileage from Paddington to Weymouth, via Swindon and Melksham. (MB 04/00)

400 ft.
300
200
100

1 in 330 | [Level] | 1 in 264 | [Level]

(site of Keinton Mandeville station, closed 1962)

(site of Charlton Mackrell station, closed 1962)

120 | 121 Milepost mileage | 122 | 123 | 124

120 | 121 | 122 | 123 miles from London | 124

CHARLTON MACKRELL : Two grimy locomotives (47211+47335) double head 6O92, the 1035 Exeter Riverside to Dollands Moor, seen passing Charlton Mackrell with a train of china clay bound for the Continent. The site of the former goods yard is to the right of the locomotives. (SM 09/98)

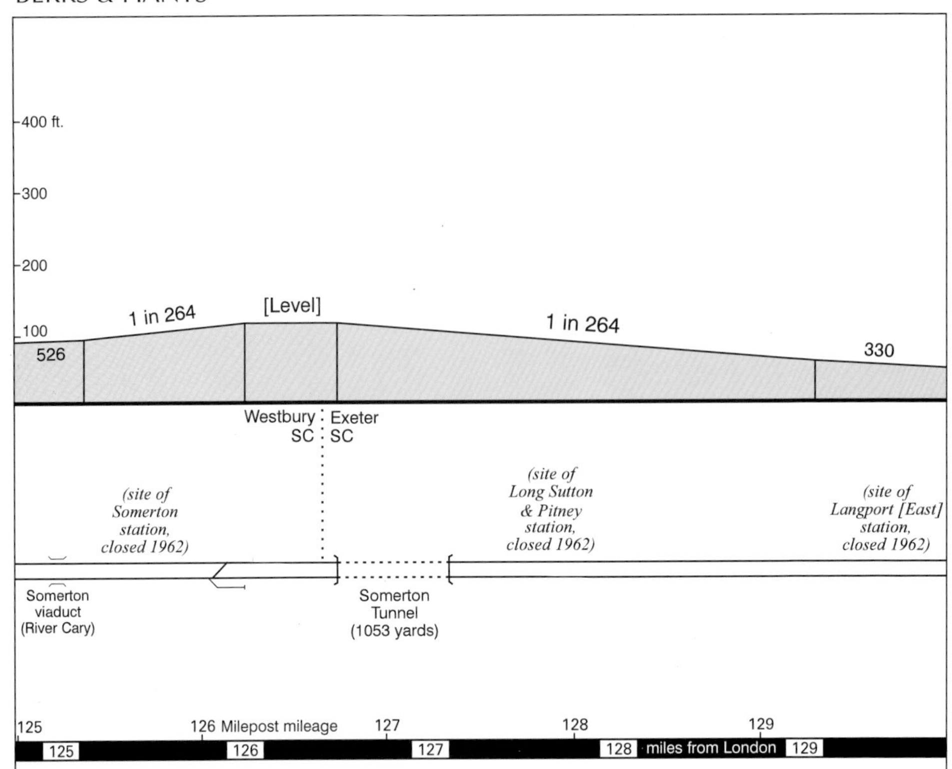

SOMERTON : The 'Berks & Hants' is remarkably devoid of architectural structures and there are only three viaducts and one tunnel on the entire route. An unidentified HST emerges from the east portal of Somerton Tunnel with 1A39, the 0634 Penzance to Paddington; the 'down' line being completely cast in shadow thus making photography at this location particularly difficult. (MB 04/00)

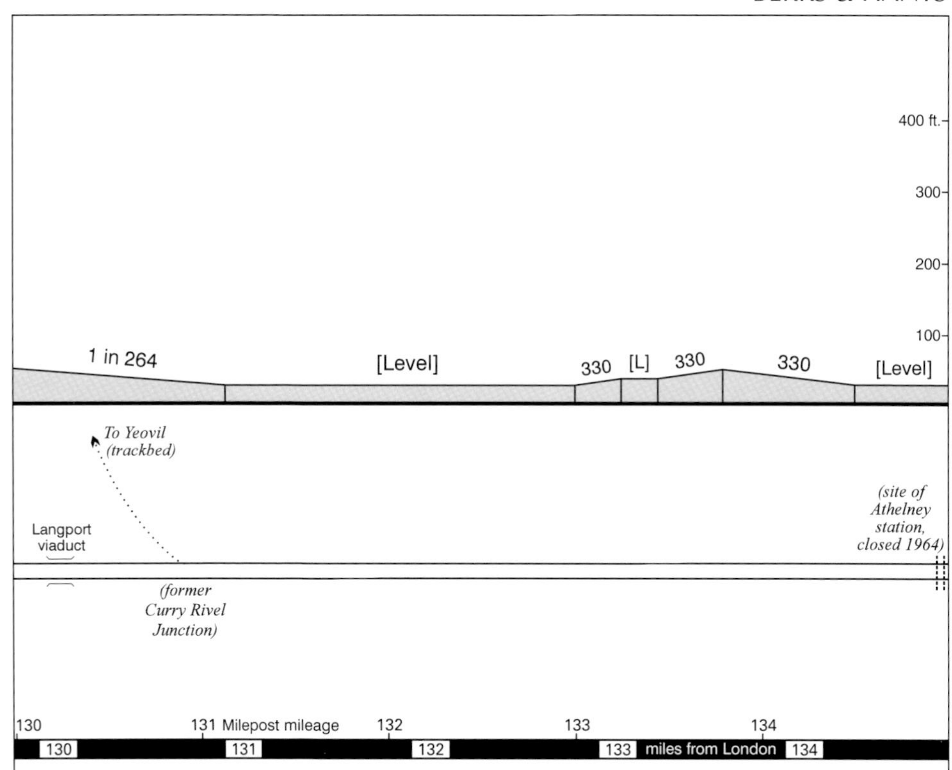

CURRY RIVEL : A minor road from Curry Rivel to Stathe crosses the main line near Oath, where the overbridge provides an excellent vantage point for photography. Unfortunately, diesel-hauled services on the stretch of line between Westbury and Taunton are scarce, to say the least! However, at the time of writing, there is a regular freight service which runs every Monday and this is seen here being hauled by 66029; 6O92, the 1016 Exeter to Dollands Moor. (MB 04/00)

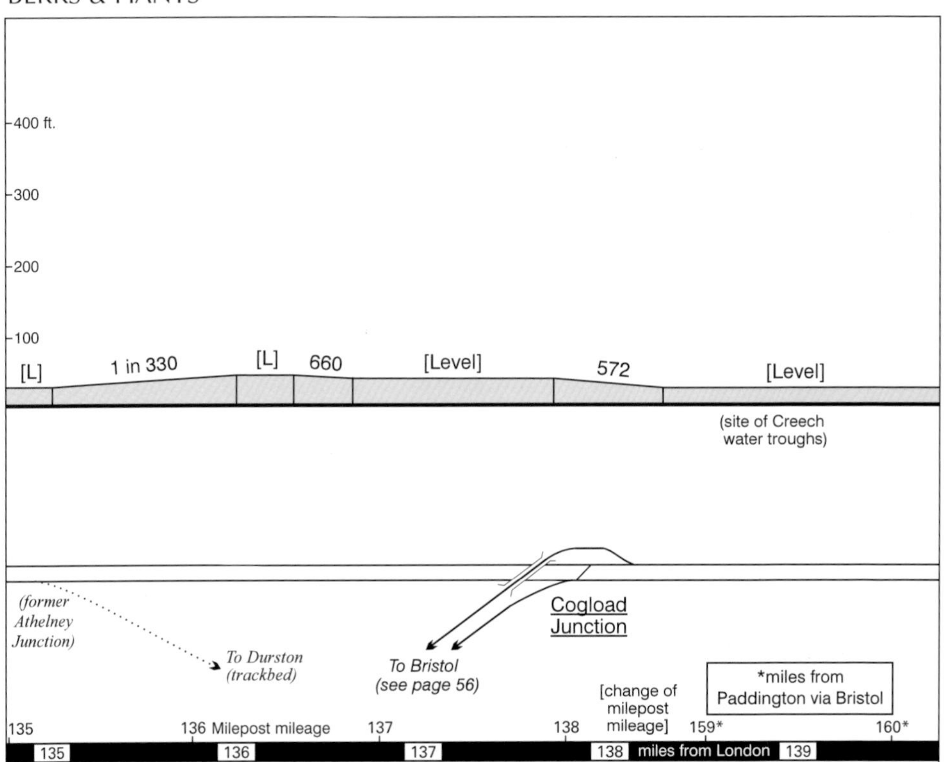

COGLOAD : Our journey down the 'Berks & Hants' eventually comes to an end when we meet up with the Great Western main line at Cogload Junction. The girder bridge which carries the 'down' main line from Bristol to Taunton over the 'Berks & Hants' is visible in the distance, as an HST heads away from Cogload with 1A46, the 0808 Penzance to Paddington. (DM 05/98)

Glossary

Miles and Chains

These tables set out the mileage for the Great Western Main Line in the 'down' direction from London Paddington to Penzance via Bristol Temple Meads, plus the 'Berks & Hants'.

Cumulative Mileage is given in Miles and Chains plus the **Local Mileage** when local mileposts replace the cumulative ones besides the running lines. Every station, junction and tunnel is listed under **Location**; stations are highlighted in bold typeface along with a note of the **Page Number** for reference.

1. LONDON PADDINGTON to PENZANCE (*via* Bristol Temple Meads)

Cumulative Mileage (M. Ch)	*Local Mileage* (M. Ch)	*Location*	*Page Number*
0. 05		**LONDON PADDINGTON**	**14**
2. 62		*Old Oak East Junction*	
3. 20		*Old Oak West Junction*	
4. 16		*Acton East Junction*	
4. 21		**Acton Main Line**	**14**
5. 56		**Ealing Broadway**	**17**
6. 46		**West Ealing**	**17**
6. 54		*West Ealing Junction*	
7. 19		*Hanwell Junction*	
7. 28		**Hanwell**	**17**
9. 06		**Southall**	**17**
9. 70		*Southall West Junction*	
10. 71		**Hayes & Harlington**	**18**
11. 07		*Heathrow Airport Junction*	
13. 17		**West Drayton**	**18**
14. 60		**Iver**	**19**
16. 18		**Langley**	**19**
18. 36		**SLOUGH**	**19**
20. 77		**Burnham**	**20**
22. 39		**Taplow**	**20**
24. 19		**Maidenhead**	**20**
31. 01		**Twyford**	**22**
35. 40		*Reading New Junction*	
35. 78		**READING**	**25**
36. 17		*Westbury Line Junction*	
36. 76		*Reading West Junction*	
38. 52		**Tilehurst**	**25**
41. 43		**Pangbourne**	**26**
44. 60		**Goring & Streatley**	**26**
48. 37		**Cholsey**	**27**
52. 66		*Didcot East Junction*	
53. 10		**DIDCOT PARKWAY**	**28**
53. 13		*Didcot West Junction*	
53. 55		*Foxhall Junction*	

(M. Ch)	(M. Ch)	Location	Page
74. 48		*South Marston Junction*	
76. 32		*Highworth Junction*	
77. 23		**SWINDON**	**34**
77. 36		*Swindon Junction*	
83. 07		*Wootton Bassett Junction*	
93. 76		**CHIPPENHAM**	**38**
96. 10		*Thingley Junction*	
99. 12		*Box Tunnel (east portal)*	
100. 78		*Box Tunnel (west portal)*	
101. 39		*Middle Hill Tunnel (east portal)*	
101. 48		*Middle Hill Tunnel (west portal)*	
104. 55		*Bathampton Junction*	
106. 24		*Sydney Gardens East Tunnel (east portal)*	
106. 28		*Sydney Gardens East Tunnel (west portal)*	
106. 29		*Sydney Gardens West Tunnel (east portal)*	
106. 33		*Sydney Gardens West Tunnel (west portal)*	
106. 71		**BATH SPA**	**41**
107. 72		**Oldfield Park**	**41**
108. 70		*Twerton Short Tunnel (east portal)*	
108. 72		*Twerton Short Tunnel (west portal)*	
109. 03		*Twerton Long Tunnel (east portal)*	
109. 15		*Twerton Long Tunnel (west portal)*	
111. 57		*Saltford Tunnel (east portal)*	
111. 65		*Saltford Tunnel (west portal)*	
113. 63		**Keynsham**	**44**
115. 58		*St. Annes Park No. 3 Tunnel (east portal)*	
116. 25		*St. Annes Park No. 3 Tunnel (west portal)*	
116. 41		*St. Annes Park No. 2 Tunnel (east portal)*	
116. 48		*St. Annes Park No. 2 Tunnel (west portal)*	
117. 46		*North Somerset Junction*	
117. 50		*Feeder Bridge Junction*	
118. 02		*Bristol East Junction*	
118. 31		**BRISTOL TEMPLE MEADS**	**45**
118. 58		*Bristol West Junction*	
119. 22		**Bedminster**	**45**
120. 15		**Parson Street**	**46**
120. 28		*Parson Street Junction*	
123. 61		*Flax Bourton Tunnel (east portal)*	
123. 66		*Flax Bourton Tunnel (west portal)*	
126. 33		**Nailsea and Blackwell**	**49**
130. 28		**Yatton**	**50**
134. 42		**Worle**	**51**
135. 11		*Worle Junction*	
138. 04		*Uphill Junction*	
145. 25		**Highbridge & Burnham**	**54**
151. 47		**Bridgwater**	**55**
158. 50		Cogload Junction	
163. 12		**TAUNTON**	**57**
164. 60		*Norton Fitzwarren Junction*	
173. 13		*Whiteball Tunnel (east portal)*	
173. 63		*Whiteball Tunnel (west portal)*	
177. 28		**TIVERTON PARKWAY**	**60**
192. 52		*Cowley Bridge Junction*	
193. 72		**EXETER ST. DAVIDS**	**63**
194. 66		**Exeter St. Thomas**	**64**

(M. Ch)	(M. Ch)	Location	Page
195.11		*Exeter Railway Junction*	
202. 36		**Starcross**	**67**
204. 37		**Dawlish Warren**	**67**
206. 07		**DAWLISH**	**68**
206. 34		*Kennaway Tunnel (east portal)*	
206. 43		*Kennaway Tunnel (west portal)*	
206. 53		*Coryton Tunnel (east portal)*	
206. 63		*Coryton Tunnel (west portal)*	
206. 66		*Phillot Tunnel (east portal)*	
206. 69		*Phillot Tunnel (west portal)*	
206. 72		*Clerk's Tunnel (east portal)*	
206. 75		*Clerk's Tunnel (west portal)*	
207. 19		*Parson's Tunnel (east portal)*	
207. 42		*Parson's Tunnel (west portal)*	
208. 70		**TEIGNMOUTH**	**68**
213. 75		*Heathfield Branch Junction*	
214. 05		**NEWTON ABBOT**	**69**
215. 09		*Aller Junction*	
217. 63		*Dainton Tunnel (east portal)*	
217. 76		*Dainton Tunnel (west portal)*	
222. 47		*Ashburton Junction*	
222. 66		**TOTNES**	**71**
227. 62		*Marley Tunnels (east portal)*	
228. 22		*Marley Tunnels (west portal)*	
231. 58		*Wrangation Tunnel (east portal)*	
231. 61		*Wrangation Tunnel (west portal)*	
234. 27		**Ivybridge**	**73**
242. 69		*Tavistock Junction*	
244. 02		*Laira Junction*	
244. 35		*Lipson Junction*	
245. 32		*Mutley Tunnel (east portal)*	
245. 46		*Mutley Tunnel (west portal)*	
245. 75		**PLYMOUTH**	**78**
247. 15	248. 28	**Devonport**	**78**
247. 24	248. 37	*Devonport Tunnel (east portal)*	
247. 29	248. 42	*Devonport Tunnel (west portal)*	
247. 47	248. 60	**Dockyard**	**78**
248. 12	249. 25	**Keyham**	**78**
248. 28	249. 41	*Dockyard Junction*	
248. 67	250. 00	*St. Budeaux Junction*	
249. 02	250. 15	**St. Budeaux Ferry Road**	**78**
250. 13	251. 26	**Saltash**	**79**
252. 74	254. 07	*Wivelscombe Tunnel (east portal)*	
253. 14	254. 27	*Wivelscombe Tunnel (west portal)*	
255. 15	256. 28	**St. Germans**	**80**
260. 48	261. 61	**Menheniot**	**82**
263. 53	264. 66	*Liskeard Junction*	
263. 58	**264. 71**	**LISKEARD**	**82**
272. 70	**274. 03**	**BODMIN PARKWAY**	**84**
274. 03	275. 16	*Brown Queen Tunnel (east portal)*	
274. 07	275. 20	*Brown Queen Tunnel (west portal)*	
276. 23	**277. 36**	**LOSTWITHIEL**	**85**
276. 41	277. 54	*Fowey Branch Junction*	
278. 06	279. 19	*Treverrin Tunnel (east portal)*	
278. 31	279. 44	*Treverrin Tunnel (west portal)*	

(M. Ch)	(M. Ch)	Location	Page
280. 53	**281. 66**	**PAR**	**86**
285. 13	**286. 26**	**ST. AUSTELL**	**89**
287. 13	288. 26	*Burngullow Junction*	
296. 37	297. 50	*Polperro Tunnel (east portal)*	
296. 63	297. 76	*Polperro Tunnel (west portal)*	
297. 77	299. 10	*Buckshead Tunnel (east portal)*	
298. 12	299. 25	*Buckshead Tunnel (west portal)*	
299. 50	**300. 63**	**TRURO**	**91**
300. 12	301. 25	*Penwithers Junction*	
308. 49	309. 62	*Redruth Tunnel (east portal)*	
308. 51	309. 64	*Redruth Tunnel (west portal)*	
308. 55	**309. 68**	**REDRUTH**	**93**
312. 27	**313. 40**	**CAMBOURNE**	**94**
318. 18	**319. 31**	**HAYLE**	**95**
319. 65	**320. 78**	**ST. ERTH**	**95**
323. 79	325. 12	*Long Rock*	
325. 37	**326. 50**	**PENZANCE**	**96**

2. The 'BERKS & HANTS.'

Cumulative Mileage	*Local Mileage*	*Location*	*Page Number*
(M. Ch)	**(M. Ch)**		
0. 05		**LONDON PADDINGTON**	**14**
35. 78		**READING**	**110**
36. 17		Westbury Line Junction	
36. 67		Oxford Road Junction	
36. 75		**Reading West**	**110**
37. 62		*Southcote Junction*	
41. 22		**Theale**	**112**
44. 63		**Aldermaston**	**112**
46. 59		**Midgham**	**113**
49. 45		**Thatcham**	**113**
52. 31		**Newbury Racecourse**	**114**
53. 06		**Newbury**	**114**
58. 38		**Kintbury**	**116**
61. 43		**Hungerford**	**117**
66. 33		**Bedwyn**	**118**
75. 26		**Pewsey**	**120**
94. 45		*Heywood Road Junction*	
94. 77		*Westbury East Loop Junction*	
95. 48	**109. 64**	**WESTBURY**	**124**
97. 02	111. 18	*Fairwood Junction*	
100. 28	114. 44	*Clink road Junction*	
102. 21	116. 37	*Blatchbridge Junction*	
106. 29	120. 45	*Witham East Somerset Junction*	
111. 73	126. 09	**Bruton**	**129**
115. 29	**129. 45**	**Castle Cary**	**130**
115. 32	115. 32	*Castle Cary Junction*	
126. 59	126. 59	*Somerton Tunnel (east portal)*	
127. 27	127. 27	*Somerton Tunnel (west portal)*	
138. 30	158. 50	*Cogload Junction*	
142. 72	**163. 12**	**TAUNTON**	**57**

Acknowledgements

The map extracts in the 'Gallery' are kindly reproduced from the following Landranger 1 : 50 00 scale Ordnance Survey maps by permission of Ordnance Survey on behalf of the Controller of He Majesty's Stationary Office, © Crown Copyright MC0100028152:

Sheet Number	Landranger Map Title	Date
174	Newbury & Wantage	1999
192	Exeter & Sidmouth	2000
200	Newquay & Bodmin	1999
201	Plymouth & Launceston	1997

The photographers who have contributed material for this book are named below along with a not of their initials, which have been used throughout in the captions for the purpose of accreditation.

Brian Aston (BA)
Richard Davies (RD)
Peter Howard (PH)
Brian Morrison (BM)
Brian Beer (BB)
Richard Giles (RG)
Steve McMullin (SM)
Ron Westwater (RW)
Martin Buck (MB)
Mike Goodfield (MG
Dave Mitchell (DM

Brief details of the non-captioned photographs are as follows:

Page	Location	Description	By
6	Knighton	43175 : 1C34, 1215 Paddington – Bristol	MB (04/00)
13	Sonning	59002 : 6V18, 1239 Hither Green – Whatley	MB (09/00)
97	Dawlish	47814 : 1M56, 1030 Paignton – Manchester	MB (09/97)
109	Westbury	59002 : 7V67, 1033 Sevington – Merehead	MB (08/00)
135	Didcot East Jct	47712 : 1O71, 0736 Blackpool – Portsmouth Hbr.	MB (09/99)

Bibliography

Railway Track Diagrams (Great Western) : Quail Map Company ISBN 1-898319-39-
Atlas of the GWR : Wild Swan Publications ISBN 1-874103-38-
Rail Atlas (GB & Ireland) : Haynes Publishing ISBN 0-86093-534-
Gradient Profiles : Ian Allan Ltd ISBN 0-7110-0875-
*Freightmaster** : Freightmaster Publishing ISSN 1357-4841
*Class One** : Freightmaster Publishing ISSN 1465-6973

* various editions used to identify/confirm train identification in the photographic content.

Also, the following cab ride videos of the route from Video 125 are highly recommended:

HST Great West (Paddington – Bristol – Exeter)
HST West (Exeter – Saltash)
HST Far West (Saltash – Penzance)